Be a Better Boss

All profits go directly to the Moondance Foundation,
set up by Henry and his family.

BE A BETTER BOSS

Learn to build great teams and lead any organization to success

HENRY ENGELHARDT

First published in Great Britain in 2021 by Moondance Foundation
This edition published in Great Britain in 2023 by
Henry Engelhardt, in partnership with whitefox publishing

www.wearewhitefox.com

ISBN 978-1-915635-25-9
Also available as an eBook and Audiobook
eBook ISBN 978-1-915635-26-6
Audiobook ISBN 978-1-915635-27-3

Cover and interior design by Couper Street Type Co.
Illustrations by John Kascht
Project management by whitefox
Printed and bound in Great Britain by Clays Ltd, Elcograf S.p.A.

To Diane, teammate for life. No Diane, no book.
(In more ways than one!)

To David and Andrew. We did good,
and had a lot of laughs along the way.

To everyone who works, or has worked, for Admiral.
Thanks for working so hard every day to make
Admiral the great company it is.

Be a Better Boss

The secret recipe of how Henry created one of the top places to work in the world and a FTSE 100 company from scratch where fun, camaraderie, ethics, diversity and results go hand-in-hand and, in fact, reinforce each other. It is a practical guide to becoming an inspiring leader, spiced up with an arsenal of stories and simple but powerful examples that will resonate with you. Once you interiorize these concepts, your leadership style and impact will never be the same. I am so grateful he wrote up his philosophy in a single book that we now distribute to every manager in Admiral to inspire more leaders and make the world a better place to work in.

Milena Mondini
CEO, Admiral Group plc

It's difficult not to be inspired by Henry's approach to running a business. His passion for clients and employees is something that should challenge and encourage all of us, regardless of business sector.

David Durlacher
CEO, Julius Baer International Limited

In his no-nonsense, approachable fashion, Henry shares a number of relevant pointers related to everything from creating and maintaining the right culture to innovation and growing bottom line, accompanying each one with relatable examples.

His humor, eloquence, and knowledge about how to build a sustainable, thriving, one-of-a-kind business has been appreciated by everyone on my team. We quote Henry when discussing strategic decisions and issues of the day.

Pina Albo
CEO, Hamilton Insurance Group

This is a book all leaders should read. Henry generously shares his thoughts, insights and experiences in a way that is accessible to everyone. He tells some real-life stories that make it an incredibly valuable and easy-to-read book. We can all learn from it and challenge our own leadership style and actions.

Annette Court
Chair of W H Smith

Not only do I give Henry's book to everyone in Confused.com but I give it to anyone I meet who is interested in being a better leader.

Louise O'Shea
Ex-CEO, Confused.com

Henry is a frequent guest speaker in my MBA classes at INSEAD France and IESE Spain. His talks on leadership and management are immensely popular. Drawing from his personal experience as founder and CEO of Admiral, Henry describes his unique approach to managing a team, growing a business and instilling a winning company culture. While his own journey has been extremely successful, he modestly inspires his audience by declaring "If I can do it, you can do it."

Henry's credibility and authenticity are unparalleled, bolstered by data describing Admiral's financial performance and Admiral team members' feedback. It is always a pleasure to observe the rapt attention of multi-cultural, multi-ethnic, multi-functional MBA students during Henry's talks.

Professor Steve Haslett, INSEAD

I have over 1,000 managers in my business and I would love it if every one of them read this book. The book is a must for new managers, but every manager can learn from all the practical tips. I also love that it is so easy to read.

Cristina Nestares
CEO, Admiral UK

CONTENTS

FOREWORD

Why am I taking the trouble to put in writing some of the things I've learned in my 40-plus years of leadership and management?

I want to see a world of great leaders and managers. There's an incredible buzz that comes from running a team, running a department, leading an operation or an organization. There's an adrenaline rush when you're needed and you know that what you *think*, what you *do*, makes a difference to so many people. I want to help you find your best leader/manager self. I want you to be a *great* leader; a *great* manager.

For me, the essence of a business career is having the opportunity, and the responsibility, to help so many people: customers, employees, partners, suppliers, stakeholders—everyone. The pressure is on you to do that well, to push yourself so that even you are surprised by the results. You owe it to those around you, sure, but you get a take-home benefit, too: the astounding feeling of self-satisfaction that comes with success.

I love business. I love leading and managing. I love the intellectual stimulation, the emotional highs and lows, the constant challenge to improve. I love helping others to achieve their goals. It's a nonstop thrill ride—and if you do it well, you exit with a fantastic sense of satisfaction. I want to share this dopamine high with you.

There's another reason I've written this book. There are a lot of lousy managers and leaders out there. The other side of the coin. Bad managers and leaders make bad decisions and those bad decisions put jobs and organizations at risk. Bad managers and leaders make those around them miserable. To have an ego-centric, uncaring boss isn't fair. It's nigh on impossible if you're unhappy in your job to then go home, flick a switch, and suddenly be a happy camper. If this book can help even a few people to be better managers then it will be a success.

I've had some really bad bosses (some stories yet to come!) and my kids have had some terrible bosses, too. One of my daughters worked in a job where the boss was often yelling, always had to prove he was the smartest person in the room, and incessantly demanded responses to emails in the evening and at weekends. We watched as my daughter's persona went from bubbly and engaged to gloomy and anxious. Her boyfriend said she was like a light bulb with the dimmer switch slowly being turned down.

After less than a year she took the big step to find a new job, even though she knew this would not look good on her CV. She was so keen to leave that she took a 30 percent pay cut for a job in a company that had a much better management reputation. Now she is thriving. Her boss is brilliant, the company is doing well, and she's involved, works hard, and gets a lot of satisfaction from her work. She's even had a couple of promotions. She got the job just as the world was going into Covid lockdown, so for the first year or more she never worked in the company's offices, nor met most of the people she worked with. Despite this unfortunate beginning with the company, having good leadership has meant a huge amount to her life and that of her boyfriend. (Note: Proof that great management can be achieved even at a distance!) The bulb is burning brightly again.

The bad boss not only affected my daughter, but her boyfriend, her parents, possibly her friends and roommates as well. Now maybe that boss works with 20 people—that would mean he is able to negatively affect between 20 and 100 people! As a leader you have a choice: you have the opportunity to help people and make their day or you can ruin the lives of an entire village!

In the course of your career as a manager you'll do a lot of managing. But do you ever take the time to really think about managing? That's what I hope to stimulate. Why not start now? Put a date in your diary for next week that just says ,"Think about management." And again for two weeks after that, and so on. Go ahead, I'll wait.

If you're going to be a manager you might as well be a *great* manager, don't you agree? Thinking about what makes great leaders and great managers is the first step in giving yourself a chance to be one of them. But no one can write you into being a great leader or manager. You have to do that yourself.

This manual should give you confidence. I had some success in my career before starting Admiral, but Admiral is my real claim to fame. Admiral grew market value from zero to billions; a handful of staff to over 10,000; zero income to almost £4 billion; profits over 30 years in the billions… I was the founder and original CEO and held that role until I decided to step down 25 years later.

I went to a good high school and did well but was nowhere near top of my class. I went to a fine, but not elite, university and, again, did well but was not at the top of my class. I went to an excellent business school but didn't make the Dean's List. In the business world, I have made many mistakes, done a lot of things badly and yet, somehow, I managed to accomplish a lot. You see where this is going? I am not extraordinary, yet I've been able to create and work with a team to grow a company from scratch to a big business—one that wins award after award for being a great company to work for. Most important is that I achieved all this without losing sight of what's really important: I managed to have breakfast and dinner with my family most mornings and evenings.

FOREWORD

If I can do it, you can do it!

I am a much better manager now than I was 30 years ago. Or 20 years ago. Or even 10 years ago. Perhaps even better than yesterday. Learning through experience, curiosity, and observation over time has helped improve my leadership and management skills. If you take this manual seriously it can open you up to new possibilities and shave time off your learning curve.

If there was a formula for manufacturing great managers and leaders, life would be easy. We'd all just read that formula and, voilà, the world would be overflowing with them. Sorry, it doesn't work that way. Here's another sorry thing: No single book or manual is going to make you a great manager or leader (not even this one!). Management and leadership are darned difficult to do well, much less to do *great*, and an entire library of books won't make you a great leader.

You have to do it yourself. You have to put the time in, you have to learn at every stage and... wait for it... you have to constantly think about it. (You put that in your diary, right?)

There is no formula, because everyone is different. We can all read the same advice but interpret and implement it differently, because each of us has our own character and history. So, as you read this manual, don't think, "How can I be like Henry?" Rather, think, "How can I learn from Henry's experiences to be a better me?" If my experiences get you thinking about your own management style—how you make decisions, how you treat people, how you think about problems, how you tackle challenges—then you'll be better at it on your own terms. I want you, every now and again, to look at yourself and what you're doing. To reflect, to consider, to assess, and to wake up and smell the management hummus.

★

FOREWORD

Great management is non-stop; great managers give all they have every day; great managers realize that the minute they get near the office in the morning they need to flick on the internal energy switch because there's no time to lose—this day is going to fly by and there are a hundred things to do!

But let's go back a half-step. Why is great management so difficult? Why can't you just ask Alexa or Google how to be a great manager? Don't read on until you've tried to answer this one. (And no, don't bother asking Alexa.)

The answer: Everything is different. Always. And always changing. Every person, every place, every situation. Things are different, and in an hour they are going to be differently different. The people you manage are different from the ones I manage, are different from the ones imaginary Bob manages. If everyone has different ingredients, there can't be one recipe. I'll add some pepper while you'll throw in Tabasco.

There's another thing that's different: you. You're different. Sorry—that's not meant in a pejorative way. You're different from me, you're different from the manager in the team next door, you're different from good ol' imaginary Bob. You think differently, you act differently, there are things that make you mad that would make me laugh, there are times you'd stand up when I'd sit down. You can't escape it: You're you and you're the core ingredient in you as a manager.

Don't worry, I'll be offering more than the stunning observation that we're all different. But that obvious thought is what makes management damn difficult. It's why a formula won't work. This manual doesn't pretend to be *the* guide to management; it's just another tool. My advice: Use as many tools as you can. Read other books, listen to podcasts, talk with people who have been there/done that, people who are growing into their roles, people who are being managed, people who have failed, semi-retired ex-CEOs...

In the following pages, as I share a few of my values and the things I stand for, remember that these are mine, not yours. Keep your grubby hands off! You need to define your own values; what you stand for. I jest. You can use any of my ingredients you like. If you need the proverbial cup of management sugar to be *great*, please knock on my door and borrow some.

Here's a promise to all managers and leaders: You'll have many moments of frustration, apprehension, uncertainty, insecurity, and that anxious feeling you get when the sky is falling. Plus acid indigestion. And that's if you do the job well!

Yes, great management is really hard to achieve but I can also promise you this: When you succeed and become a great manager, you'll get a satisfaction that is more rewarding than any bonus or other reward you might imagine. Leading other people to do great things, helping them become better than they ever thought they'd be, winning as a team, will all make you feel fantastic. Those moments can support you in your old age. (Trust me, I speak from experience on that one!)

So, yes, I hope this manual stimulates you to think about leadership and management. But the cerebral bit plus £2.50 (with a contactless card) will get you on the London Underground. *You* still have to get on with it and do the heavy lifting. It will be challenging, but don't be daunted.

I promise you, you'll be amazed by what you can achieve. *You can do this. YOU can be GREAT.*

Good luck.

—Henry
Cardiff, Wales, 2023

Four key Henry-isms

(to be explained within).

•

If people like what they do, they'll do it better.

•

The power of the team is invariably greater
than the power of any single individual.

•

You can never fully appreciate how important
you are to the people you manage.

•

You can't hit your targets yourself.

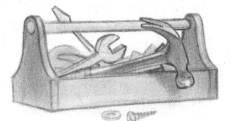

USING THIS MANUAL

This book is divided into four main parts, and concludes with…
a conclusion! Each part has a bunch of chapters, and along the
way you'll find quick lists of takeaways. I'd call them lessons, but
that sounds pretentious and deadly dull. The idea of a practical
"takeaway" is what I intend—a tip that you can take to the office
and use the next day.

Part 1 is where you'll hear some stories about my work history,
how Admiral got started, and some of what I've learned over the
past half-century. Every experience is a learning experience; here
are some of mine.

Part 2 is more on the philosophical side of leadership and management. But it's got stories, too!

Part 3 What do you need to do to be a great leader/manager? I've
reduced this to just three things. If you read nothing else but want
to get some value from this book, read this section.

Part 4 is something of a Gatling gun of practical things I've learned over many years that might help you as you go along. I don't expect every one of these to be relevant to every reader. Pick the ones that might help you.

The Conclusion is a summary and a personal note. If you're the type to read the end of a book first, this is perfect for you! (But promise you'll go back later and read some of the great stories that can help you be a better manager.)

Why should you listen to anything I say?

I'll cut right to the chase. There is a lot of good experience I can pass on from my entire 50-year working life. But the key to my credibility is the success of starting up and running Admiral Group plc. I was hired to set up and run Admiral in the middle of 1991 and stepped down as CEO in May 2016. There will be more about the creation, development and growing pains of Admiral later.

As I mentioned in the Foreword, for those who don't know (outrageous!), Admiral is a UK company that has gone from startup to a value in excess of £9 billion (about $12 billion). All the growth has been organic. Admiral has made billions in profits and paid billions in dividends along the way. At the time of writing my family and our family charitable foundation still own circa 14 percent of the company.

They say a chart is worth a thousand words, so here are three charts that show you what a success Admiral has been. The first shows Admiral's turnover, second is Admiral's profits, and the third the evolution of the share price since we went public in 2004.

USING THIS MANUAL

Group Turnover (£m)

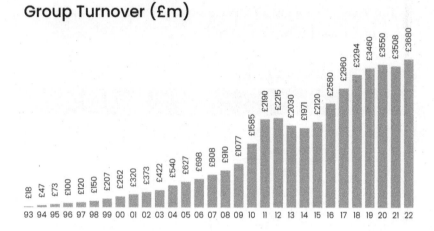

£18	£47	£73	£100	£120	£150	£207	£262	£320	£373	£422	£540	£627	£698	£808	£910	£1077	£1585	£2190	£2215	£2030	£1971	£2120	£2580	£2960	£3294	£3460	£3550	£3508	£3680
93	94	95	96	97	98	99	00	01	02	03	04	05	06	07	08	09	10	11	12	13	14	15	16	17	18	19	20	21	22

Group Share of Profit (£m)

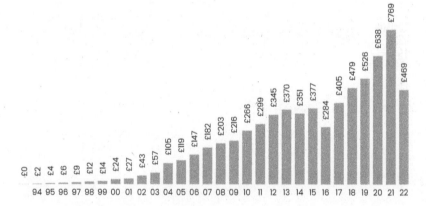

£0	£3	£4	£6	£9	£12	£14	£24	£27	£43	£57	£105	£119	£147	£182	£203	£216	£266	£299	£345	£370	£351	£377	£284	£405	£479	£526	£693	£769	£469
94	95	96	97	98	99	00	01	02	03	04	05	06	07	08	09	10	11	12	13	14	15	16	17	18	19	20	21	22

Group Share Price (Sep 04—Dec 22)

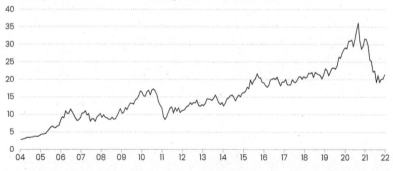

But wait—it's not just about economics. Here's a slide that shows a few of the awards we've won or lists we've been included in.

Great Places to Work

Awards, by Country		2022
United Kingdom		4th
Canada	Halifax	4th
Italy	ConTe	4th
Spain	Admiral Seguros	2nd
France	L'olivier	7th
US	Elephant	GPTW accredited
	Compare	GPTW accredited
India	Admiral Technologies	GPTW accredited
	Admiral Solutions	35th
Europe		19th

Best Companies

Admiral is the only company to make this list every year since the award began in 2001.

- 2nd Best Big Company to Work For 2022
- Best Companies to Work For Special Award 2022—Wellbeing—1st
- Best Companies to Work For Special Award 2022—Giving Something Back
- Best Companies to Work For Special Award 2022—Learning and Development
- Best Companies to Work For in Wales 2022—9th
- Best Insurance Company to Work For in the UK 2022—3rd
- Britain's Most Admired Companies—Britain's Most Admired Insurer—1st

USING THIS MANUAL

In the Appendix (page 288) is a list of company honors we've won. Almost all of them have something to do with being a great place to work. My favorite, even more than being the 14th best workplace in the world (this world!) is our inclusion in the *Sunday Times* Best Companies to Work For list every year that list has been compiled! We are the only company to be in the list every year. So when the question comes up at your family's Christmas trivia competition, don't answer Google, don't answer Bain Consulting, don't answer We Work or McDonald's or Marks & Spencer, because the right answer is Admiral Group. It's a company that lives in a commodity-like industry, with dozens of competitors, where the average salary of the 11,000 people who work there is much closer to an average wage than six digits. It's a place where people want to work; a place where people wake up in the morning not in dread of going to the office, but looking forward to a day at work.

So, on the one hand you have great financial results and on the other you have many awards for being a great employer. The savvy reader will have already realized that these are not two independent pieces of information. The beauty is in the realization that being a great place to work greatly enhances your chances of delivering brilliant economic results.

The upshot of all this is that almost everything I talk about in this book is something I've tried and that has worked, either for me, or for those around me, or both. (Or maybe didn't work!) When I talk about things like putting staff first, having fun at work, and so on, I'm saying those things because they work. Admiral proves it. These aren't laboratory tests, they aren't hypotheses answered by an educational paper—these are actual life situations that happened.

This book is home to many things they won't teach you in any school. They are the product of a lot of learning. You might question some of them, you might think, "Well, they wouldn't work in my business/industry/country." And I'm sure, in some instances, that's right. Not everything in this book will work for everyone, everywhere. But I believe the concepts are right. And I believe the concepts can cross all those boundaries. The other side of that coin is that there's bound to be something that *will* work for everyone.

I believe that even if you're a manager in the public sector or leading a group of people in Poughkeepsie, or whatever or wherever, much of what's in this book can work for you. That's because the main message of the book is: Use your mind; be creative; think; work as a team. And you can use your mind, be creative, think and work as a team in any business, organization, country, or industry.

Why should you listen to me? I will be the first to admit that I am not extraordinary. As I wrote in the Foreword, I went to good schools and did well, but I was not top of my class. Yet I've done pretty well. I have found that a lot of people shoot themselves down before they've even given themselves a chance. Here is a not-so-secret secret: You don't have to do everything brilliantly. In fact, you might not do *anything* brilliantly. You've just got to keep thinking, learning, and trying. Circumstances might keep you from achieving your goals but don't be your own obstacle. I hope what follows helps you in some way to be a better leader, a better manager. Let's get on with it, eh?

But first... a quick quiz

These questions will help you find the takeaways you might need in the pages that follow. Don't worry, your answers won't count toward your final grade.

USING THIS MANUAL

1. Are you a great manager?

Honest answer, please. I don't mean a good manager, a competent manager, or even a successful manager. I mean a *great* manager. Don't ask your friends or your team members. This is a judgment of you, by you.

If you can honestly answer "yes" to this question, then stop reading, give me a call and help me write the next manual. But if your answer is "not sure" or "no", please read on.

2. Do you want to be a great manager?

If your answer is "no", go back to your video game. If "yes", keep reading.

3. How will you know if you are OK, decent, good, or great? Or complete rubbish?

The journey to great starts with a bit of self-analysis. Ask yourself:

4. Who are you?
5. What do you stand for?
6. What kind of a manager and leader do you want to be?

Those last ones are three simple questions, very straightforward, but they might just paralyze you so that you never read the rest of the book! Sorry, but this is a big step in figuring out how to become a great manager.

Let me give you an example. (Told you there'd be stories.)

At the very beginning of Admiral there were five of us working on the business plan. We had office space in a dilapidated building on Borough High Street, south of London Bridge. It was a building the group that had hired us had used for another business. But they had moved that business to Haywards Heath a few years before, so the building was empty. If I'm fair, it was a bit of a tip.

This building was three storeys high and they gave us the third floor, slapped a lick of paint on the walls, threw down a carpet, and there we were. How dodgy was this place? About a month into our stay, someone broke into our office—using a fork. (They took our computer and our coffee maker. Fortunately, we had a backup of our business plan, but going without coffee was brutal!)

Sometime in the first few months I got the other four members of the team together at our group meeting area—a small round table. I told the team then that I intended to have a successful business career and a successful family life. (I had one wife and two small children at this point. I still have the one wife, but we added another two children along the way.)

I told them that I did not believe the two were mutually exclusive. I said that I would work hard and that there were certain to be some days when I was in the office long hours. But most days I planned to have breakfast with my family each morning and dinner with them in the evening.

Nowadays they call this "work–life balance". Back then it was called heresy! How could you possibly launch a business without working 20-hour days?

Today this is one of the principles Admiral Group stands on: You can be successful in the office and at home. In fact, I would go further: To really be successful you *should be* successful in the office and at home.

Questions 5 and 6 remind me of two principles that define me. First principle: It doesn't matter to me who you are, your gender, the color of your skin, your nationality, your sexual preference, your age, what God you pray to, how many tattoos or piercings you have, or what color socks you wear—all that matters is the effort you put in and the quality of your work.

I once had a young employee who was a human graffiti wall,

with piercings to match. He came up to me one day and said, "Thank you."

"You're welcome," I replied. "But what are you thanking me for?"

He said no one else would hire him. "Why?" I asked.

He lifted his hands, palms out, showing me his arms. He had rings in his ears, nose, one eyebrow, etc. I asked him if he did a good job. He said he did. End of conversation. Why should I care about his tattoos and piercings?

Second principle: Every member of staff should treat every other member of staff with dignity and respect at all times. No exceptions, no excuses. You will have times when you're frustrated with a colleague, or even downright angry, but that is not an excuse for treating someone badly in the office. I'll come back to this one later.

These are some of the principles of who I am and how I define myself. They create lines that cannot be crossed. There is no being half-pregnant on these things. And so I ask you to consider, as you read along:

7. What are your values?
8. Where are your uncrossable lines?

You cannot be great if you're a hypocrite. I learned this the hard way—not because I'm a converted hypocrite, but because I've had the displeasure of working for hypocrites. Pretty obvious statement, right? But you might be surprised (perhaps not!) at how many people, especially when they move into positions of management, have one set of rules for themselves (and possibly a few selected others) and a different set of rules and standards for everybody else.

You are likely to be tempted by this yourself. Your management role may come with perks—or the chance to create self-defined perks—and you will be tempted to grab them. You'll be tempted to rationalize, "All managers get these things" or "I work so hard, I deserve these things." Or this insidious one, "Bob in Finance takes them, why shouldn't I?"

I advise you to resist temptation. It might even be your manager offering you something special, possibly because he or she wants that something special for him or herself and it looks better if others around also have it. A bigger desk, a trip abroad, more holiday days—whatever it is, resist!

If you want to earn the trust of those you manage, you need to show them that there is one set of rules and everyone, even you, must follow those rules.

Another story: I once worked for a manager who demanded that his team work hard. Yet every day, a little after 4 pm, I would watch him, briefcase in hand, walk past my office, heading to the car park. I knew he was off to the pub and that I'd be in the office for another three hours—and I'd be back at the office the next morning before he arrived.

How did he think that made me feel? What did he think would go through my mind when he talked about how everyone should work hard? (Those questions are not part of the quiz. The quiz is over, people. Relax.)

I could have left at 4 pm as well, except for two things. One was my team. I couldn't send that message to them. Two hypocrites don't make a whole. Secondly, it wouldn't have been the right thing for the business. But he made it tempting! As it happened, this came back to haunt him because his hypocrisy planted one of the many seeds of disloyalty that led to the creation of Admiral.

When you set your values and standards, whatever they are, remember that they apply to all.

USING THIS MANUAL

Why pay attention to anything I say? Don't answer that; I'll tell you. This book isn't about me, it's about you—and helping you become a great manager. In my story are things that will a) help you and b) provide you with some trust that my experience can save you a lot of angst and difficult moments on your journey to greatness. I've had enough angst and difficult moments along the way for the both of us!

Everything is a learning experience. Every day, everything. Every setback, every triumph, every story, every interaction. As a business person I am always looking at the way people present their products, the way they present themselves, why I'll buy something in one place and not another, how pricing affects my purchasing, the way a business is run, who a product is being marketed to and if it is appealing to the people it needs to appeal to. Everything.

Little experiences can mean so much to consumers. As a consummate consumer I am always analyzing my experiences and then trying to figure out how I can take the good from an experience and transplant that into one of the businesses I am involved with.

Let me give you an example. Not long ago, I was visiting the Admiral office in Seville, staying in an area I wasn't familiar with. When I'm traveling, I like to go for a little power walk first thing in the morning. There is nowhere better to do this than Seville, because the whole city is starting to wake up at 6.30 am. (And it's usually warm!) I also like to find a little coffee shop, the smaller the better, near the hotel so I can end my walk with a coffee, maybe breakfast.

On this particular day it was grey and a tad drizzly. Such luck, to get rained on in Seville! As I returned from my walk, I stopped at a tiny coffee shop I'd noticed earlier. At the window, I ordered coffee and buttered toast—the guy serving, who I assumed was the owner, helped me with my Spanish such that I learned a good word. "Mantequilla" is butter. Perfect. I sat at one of the small tables outside with my toast and coffee, people-watching.

I checked my phone for messages and news, and soon the owner opened the window and motioned to me, holding a piece of paper, which I assumed was the bill. I went to get it and—wait a minute—it wasn't the bill. What is this? Wow, it's the Wi-Fi code! The gentleman had gone out of his way to write down the code for me. I had spent about 3 euros on my breakfast, and he never knew if he would ever see me again (he did, the next morning!), but he had taken the time and trouble to help me. Observant, helpful, kind. It's not a big deal, but those little service touches make all the difference in the world. How can we translate that experience into doing similar types of things for our customers?

The point of this story and what's to follow is: Everything is a learning experience. Allow me to share some of my experiences, and what I've learned.

PART 1
HISTORY

CHAPTER 1

BURGERS AND BACKPACKS

I started working when I was 13. My first job was at Poochie's: a very small place in a strip mall on a busy street in a modestly affluent suburb of Chicago that sold hot dogs and hamburgers (don't forget the fries!). My pay was the minimum wage: $1.60/hour. At 13, it seemed a fortune—$1.60 every single hour! The beauty of Poochie's was how it approached its market. It had a powerful competitor on its doorstep, about 250 yards away: a Burger King with plenty of parking. But Poochie's was different. That differentiator was quality. Poochie's beef came from the local butcher. We blanched our own fries rather than buy pre-blanched fries (big difference!). Our tomatoes were always the ripest, our buns the freshest.

Poochie's also charged more; it was much more expensive to eat at Poochie's than at Burger King.

And yet, the queue for Poochie's burgers and hot dogs would stretch out the door. Saturdays in particular were mad. The crowds arrived before noon and it was absolutely non-stop Poochie's mania until about 3pm. Then, two hours later, it started again for Saturday supper! How did Poochie's succeed when there was a big brand name with cheaper prices practically next door?

The guy who started Poochie's was a jeweler. At first, Poochie's was his part-time job. As the business grew, he gave up being a jeweler and made Poochie's his full-time occupation. And three years or so after that he bought a big house in the suburbs with a swimming pool.

Maybe his background in jewelry accounted for his attention to detail and his insistence on quality ingredients. Whatever it was, Poochie's hit a sweet spot. Particularly with families—moms especially. Moms who didn't feel like cooking but felt a bit guilty giving their kids Burger King or McDonald's saw that Poochie's used the best ingredients. So, it cost a bit more, but hey, the family was worth it, right? And the food really was great. The kids loved it. Dads loved it even more!

I worked in a customer-facing role, taking the orders and then collecting the hamburgers or hot dogs from the grill, adding all the condiments requested, bagging the fries (great fries!), and then collecting the cash. So, besides the marketing lesson, I also had my first taste—a delicious one—of process.

What was the most efficient way to build a sandwich? Efficiency is important when there is a queue, which was most

Poochie's takeaways

- People don't always buy what's cheapest. Quality counts.
- When you start a new job, look at it with a fresh eye for efficiency.

26

of the time. Why were the fries over there and not over in the other corner? How could four of us work efficiently in a space designed for two?

Of course, it was only later in life that I realized how much learning I'd absorbed. When I was 13, I was pretty well focused on my $1.60. I worked at Poochie's for less than a year, leaving after a bit of creative bargaining that failed. Two of the other employees were brothers, both older than I was, and they conspired to make my life miserable. After several months on the job, I asked for 20 cents an hour more when I had to work a shift with them. My request was denied, and shortly thereafter my career at Poochie's ended.

Shafted in golf

I won't bore you with all of my teenage jobs. I did caddy for a number of years and that was great for exercise, golf experience, and my wallet! But more important to my business education was working for a retail golf store while I was in high school. The guy who ran it was a brilliant buyer. He understood the value of buying cheap, holding stock, selling at normal prices, and reaping the benefits of big margins.

For instance, a manufacturer would call him and say they had 250 golf bags they were trying to unload. They'd negotiate a price, say $10 each. He'd take them all, stash them in a warehouse and wheel them out a few at a time over the year and sell them for $75 each. Manufacturers who were stuck with excess stock knew to call him first. And it meant he got first choice of what was out there and could keep those great deals from his competitors. Symbiosis! These lessons in negotiation were not wasted on me.

There was also a lesson in ethics that I learned, but I only realized it was an ethics lesson some years later.

At that time, the mid-1970s, golf clubs came with two shaft options: Regular and stiff. One day a manufacturer called my boss about some excess inventory—typical, so far—and offered a great deal on them. Fifty sets of clubs with stiff shafts. Now stiff shafts are generally for very good, young golfers with fast swing speeds. Most weekend golfers use regular shafts. In fact, stiff shafts will hinder the average golfer's game. As if the game wasn't hard enough!

That's probably why the manufacturer was getting rid of the clubs—it was much harder to sell a stiff-shafted set. Stiff and regular shafts look the same, so shaft strength was indicated by a narrow label wrapped around the shaft: red for regular, black for stiff. My coworkers and I were instructed to use a razor blade to carefully remove the black bands and replace them with red ones.

Lo and behold, we now had 50 sets of very sellable regular-shafted clubs!

We were assured that no amateur golfer would tell the difference. Not that we needed a rationalization. We were told to do this, and I am sure that if we had objected on ethical grounds we would have been ethically dismissed from our jobs.

Buying a new set of golf clubs is hope personified. A golfer does it in the naïve belief that this purchase will make him or her a better golfer. It's all about the kit! But if I invested a few hundred dollars in my fantasy and found out I'd been sold a product that was not fit for purpose, I would be furious!

Decades later, this dilemma lingers in my mind—in a good way. It helps me

Golf lessons

- Buying and selling is an art. It must be practiced, but it's a talent that can make or break a business.
- Ethical dilemmas can arise anywhere, anytime. Do the right thing.
- Look at any decision through a customer's eyes.

remember to consider how the decisions the "businessperson me" makes will be judged by the "consumer me." If we all put that lens on our decision-making then I'd be confident that we'd make good decisions. Those decisions may not always be profit-maximizing in the short term, but they'd allow us to look in the mirror every morning without shame and probably be profit-maximizing in the long term.

Ethical decisions are a challenge. The situation the golf store owner put us in bothers me still, 45 years later! What he did was not just unfair to the customers, it was unfair to me. Be careful never to put others in an awkward spot like that.

How to keep a business small

My father ran a small business wholesaling beef to Chicago grocery stores and butchers. This was a brutal business: a perishable product, razor-thin margins, demanding unions—even the weather was an unpredictable variable that affected deliveries. My father did well, but it was always a small business. When I went to work for him, summers and holidays when I was in my teens, I learned the reasons why.

My father was a fantastic salesman. This was a complicated business. The beef would come in from Iowa or Texas on big semi-trailers. It arrived cut in quarters, and his operation would cut it up into smaller pieces, as demanded. Then they'd deliver it to the butchers and grocery stores, who would then cut it into the familiar portions that customers would buy.

Moving the meat through the system as quickly as possible was crucial—and that's why being a great salesman was the key. Meat dehydrates as it ages. The meat was bought and sold by weight, so if it lingered in the cooler for a couple of days, it was almost impossible to sell it for more than it cost. The sale price stayed the same but the meat now weighed less. The profit margin literally dried up.

Ensuring a steady flow of product often meant convincing customers to buy more of a certain cut. One of his bigger customers, a grocery chain, often ran a special on a particular cut of beef, placed big adverts in the newspapers, and ordered a huge quantity of that cut.

But that meant my father had to find buyers for the rest of the animal. (Remember, the beef arrived simply cut into quarters.) For decades my father would spend every evening—and Saturday mornings—at the office, calling customers, selling meat and figuring out how he was to fulfil all of his orders.

And at this he was a genius. But it also meant a very poor work–life balance. He was already on his way to work by the time the rest of the family woke up in the morning, and he'd come back through the door each evening at 9 pm, when we were saying goodnight. That's one of the reasons I started working at 13. We never took regular holidays because my father could never be out of the office for very long.

But his genius at selling was not matched by his management style. The reason his business could never grow was because he was a micro-manager whose philosophy seemed to be management-by-screaming. When he wasn't on the phone buying or selling, it seemed all he did was yell at his staff. No one could do anything right. Ever. I saw these big, tough beef luggers shrivel up in fear when they saw this little guy coming towards them. No one ever took any initiative because they had become trained to believe that anything they did would be wrong. In fact, there was a good possibility that they'd get a kicking for having done something so stupid. Everyone just waited for his orders. It was great learning. Not for them, for me.

In the course of my years I've had the displeasure of working for—or having to manage—a number of bully-managers. It took me a long time to learn that the first symptom of bully-management is that everyone else hides from responsibility and initiative. When you see this in your organization or department, think of my father's business.

So much of what I've learned is about what not to do; that what I was seeing couldn't be right, so doing the opposite must be a better way. From my father I learned that if you want to create a big business you have to unleash the potential of others. If you try to do it all yourself, you can only create something as big as you (and that's probably something pretty small). You are just one person and can be stretched only so far.

Bottom up

I attended the University of Michigan: a large, well-regarded school in the small city of Ann Arbor. I had a "double major," studying journalism as well as radio, television and film.

Although I never worked professionally as a journalist, there were big benefits to learning reporting and editing skills at Michigan. I worked for three and a half years as a sportswriter and editor on the university newspaper, the *Michigan Daily*, which truly was a daily paper (except Monday), delivered around the campus and city. This wasn't a giveaway—readers had to pay 10 cents. It was as close to working

Our student newspaper was old-school—the type was set in a hot lead-alloy slug produced on massive Linotype machines. Each "line o' type" (get it?) was created by a skilled operator at a keyboard, and the article, which might be 40 or 50 lines long (and heavy!), was dropped into a page form. The point: Extra words meant extra labor. I learned this efficiency lesson early.

31

for a "real" newspaper as you could get at a university.

Sports were big business at Michigan. The football stadium holds 110,000 people and it was, and is, filled for every game. In the 1970s tickets for the general public were $50 (students paid a reduced price) for six or seven home games a year. Do the math—this was big business.

In journalism class during the day and at the *Daily* at night, we were constantly reminded: Write so people get the message right away, with as little effort as possible. Be concise. Be clear.

An editor tells a reporter to write a story to an approximate length. In those days, well before the internet, the editor then had to fit the story on a physical page. If the story was too long for the space, the editor would not search for the odd paragraph or stray words that are most appropriate to cut—especially on deadline, after a basketball game, close to midnight. The presses downstairs were warming up! No, an editor on deadline simply cut your precious story from the bottom up. Which meant that if you'd put any significant details at the end, they might not make the paper. So the writer had to get the most important things up front and make them as easy to digest as possible. (The customer—the reader—may be in a hurry, too.)

Lo and behold, this is exactly the same approach you should use for business writing—and the rules extend to advertising. When you're writing a business report or memo, or even an email, the goal is to get people to read it.

But, just as the journalist doesn't know precisely how much space his or her story will get, you never know how much your reader will actually read. You might go crazy and write a 15-page memo, with the last three pages being a dynamic write-up of your conclusions. But your reader never gets there. The reader should get everything needed to make a good decision ("good" means the one you want him or her to make!) from that first page. If not, you haven't written it well. Think about these factors:

Brevity. That dynamic write-up of your conclusions? Start with that. Make the first sentences crystal clear and concise. You can't depend on anyone—especially a busy boss—getting further than that. Then go on to support your conclusion.

Clarity. If they do read further, will they understand what they've read? Can you take a complex subject and write so a 14-year-old could understand it? Your manager might be able to understand a complicated issue, but what if they show your paper to a manager in a different part of the company? Or the board? These people might not have the technical competence to grasp your subject. And it's unlikely that you'd get a second chance to write a simpler version. Learn to break complex ideas and information down into their simplest parts.

Priority. If your audience is to take away one, and only one, thing from your memo or presentation, what is that one thing? In the business world, if a reader comes away with one clear point from your missive, that should be considered a good result. This is your shot. Make it count. It's too easy for people to forget things—and the more you throw at them, the more they'll forget.

> ### Break the curse of the boring memo!
>
> Which of these would you rather read?
>
> "In the third quarter my team's performance was up by over 20 percent on the year before and 9.75 percent on the previous quarter, although the good weather may have had a positive effect on results."
> Or...
> "Bob's Team = UP 20 percent!! :-)"
> Powerful. Simple. Memorable.

The same goes for advertising. Personally, when I hear a complex message from a company, I end up discarding the entire message. If they had concentrated on a single, simple message, I might have been able to digest that. People are busy, and there is a lot of competition for their attention. If you can get them to remember just one single thing you've written or said, that's a triumph. Short, simple, clear. That's it.

Ever get lost listening to an IT person? Haven't we all? But I still remember—clearly!—our first IT manager at Admiral, nearly 30 years ago, trying to explain to me the differences between operating systems and the hardware they run on. A pretty complex topic. I am not an IT expert, but I can understand a bit.

He wanted me to grasp why it was usually best to use hardware and software from the same company. He said it was like putting on a pair of gloves and then putting your fist into your palm of the other hand. The gloves are a pair, so they fit together just right. Using two disparate suppliers is like wearing two different gloves. They might seem to fit together, but there will be places where they don't make a good match. This was a simple, visual metaphor that a layman could understand.

So we bought a pair of gloves: the same company for both the hardware and the operating system. Before Admiral, I was with Churchill Insurance, which opted for separate vendors. We had more problems and downtime in my first year with Churchill than we had in the first decade at Admiral. The simple, clear explanation our IT manager gave me helped lead to a good decision. If you can think of a clear, useful metaphor for a problem, use it!

Writing clearly is more valuable now than ever before. Today, nobody wants to read. We

Bullet points
- Get to the point— fast!
- Be concise.
- Be clear.
- Simplify.

are so deluged with visuals—pictures, videos, emojis, gifs—that people are losing their patience with wading through pages of text. It's why some impatient readers just skimmed the last few pages and went straight to the box.

My big mistake

I am sometimes asked, "What was your greatest mistake?" Well, it happened when I was in university. As I entered my senior year, I wanted to write a thesis for my journalism major. It wasn't required, but I wanted to show I was a serious journalist. I had done well in my radio/TV/film classes and enjoyed them—but that was Plan B.

This is near the end of the '70s, remember. Woodward and Bernstein had made journalism the flavor of the decade. I had in my mind a rather glamorous image of the journalist (heck, Robert Redford played Woodward in a movie!), as did many others. Everybody and his dog wanted to be a reporter or sportswriter (the *Daily* had 25 of us covering Michigan sports, more than were on the staff of the *Detroit Free Press*).

As I would find out, newspaper jobs were difficult to come by, and when they did happen they didn't pay very much. This was also the very beginning of the cable TV era in the US. With that came a proliferation of stations and a need for directors, cameramen, writers, performers, etc.

A couple of days before classes were to begin that September, I got a call from the head of the radio/TV/film department. They were putting together a special class on television directing and they wanted me to be in it. Whoa, Nelly! What an honor. But I started thinking that I'd never have time to dedicate myself to both that and my journalism thesis, which would take up a lot of time. So I turned it down.

Ooof. Wrong choice! Even today it hurts to think about it. The journalism thesis turned out to be a waste of time—and a lot of time at that! Long before I turned it in, I knew it was rubbish. And cable TV did indeed revolutionize broadcasting in America. I could have been at the front of the queue for the new jobs this created. The ESPN boat sailed without me!

But what really was my mistake? It was making the decision all by myself. I didn't talk to anyone about it. I didn't ask anyone for advice—not a family member, not a professor, not a fellow student, not even someone who didn't know anything about the subject (often a good idea).

Option plays

- Remember: You don't know it all.
- Find a dog and talk it through.
- Or find a person to bounce options off and then listen—to them and to yourself.

I'm sure I would have done better if I'd just told the dog what the choices were. Sadly, I didn't have a dog.

There's a great lesson here for those wanting to become great managers: Get a dog. No, the lesson is always talk decisions through with someone—anyone—before you make your call.

The mere act of talking things through may enlighten you to what is best or what you really want. I often find that reviewing things out loud flips the switch on the light bulb in my head. It's something about how the brain processes information—just as writing something down can produce new clarity or fresh thoughts. Secondly, someone else is likely to see things in a slightly different light (or a radically different light) and point out things you didn't see or think were pertinent.

Do not make the mistake I made—thinking you can see all angles and reach the right conclusion on your own. Especially for major issues. This decision shaped my entire life. I thought I knew enough to make it without any help. But I didn't. (Saying that, things didn't turn out too badly for me in the end.)

Big Macs on the Champs-Élysées

A week after graduation I left the US for Paris. I had started taking French lessons in my last year of university—part of my master plan, which included securing a summer work permit for France.

Which I got. And I promptly landed a job at a restaurant in the heart of the sophisticated City of Light—a McDonald's on the Champs-Élysées.

Why would I want to start my career with McDonald's in Paris? *Cherchez la femme!*

That's right, I went for a girl. Not just a random girl, but a particular girl. This was a decision that worked out very well because that girl and I have been married 40 years and have four great kids!

I digress.

Counter points

- When you implement a system really, really well, you can make just about anything work.
- To understand a process, imbed yourself in it.
- Mastering one particular skill can make you valuable and save your job.
- Knowing the language helps.

McDonald's is another fascinating business. It was process on steroids (cheap steroids). Where Poochie's had been bespoke sandwiches, quality ingredients and higher prices, McDonald's was precision efficiency, absolute dedication to consistency, quality ingredients and low prices. I almost didn't make it at McDonald's. I didn't speak French well and the store was run by a gruff Corsican who was built like a refrigerator. He would bark instructions at the staff all day long.

In my first or second week, he shouted an order at me. I had no idea what he was on about, so I did the instinctive thing and grabbed a rag, came out from behind the counter, and started wiping off tables. Clever, eh? One of the few employees who spoke English came up to me and said, "Er, he asked you to go downstairs and bring up the ice." Oh. I knew that.

Remember this: In any business—even making burgers—it always helps to know how to do one thing really well. In my case, I was saved by my ability to apply special sauce to buns at an extraordinary pace to keep up with the Turkish grill man, who, thankfully, spoke some English. We made a good team and served up hundreds of burgers every day. I did this for a few months before leaving to travel. I'm not sure how they ever got the special sauce on the buns after I left.

It was a worthwhile few months. McDonald's gave me great insight into how a machine works from the best possible vantage point: Inside the machine.

Budget travel and priceless lessons

With my hard-earned McDonald's wages in my pocket, my French girlfriend and I loaded our backpacks and traveled for the next seven or eight months: Africa, Europe, the Middle East. I spent a few months picking grapefruits on a kibbutz in Israel (great fun!).

A number of years later, when we were married and in our late twenties, we put on our backpacks again and went off to Asia and Australasia. That trip came several years into our careers, after much discussion. My mother was concerned that we would be unemployable when we returned.

It turned out to be one of the best decisions of our lives.

We met fantastic people and saw amazing things. Traveling like this also proved to be a good way to understand ourselves. There is satisfaction in living on a budget and out of a backpack for

Travel souvenirs
- People are different and see things differently.
- Tolerate those differences.
- Choose a good traveling companion!

months. We stayed at hotels costing as little as a dollar a night (Christmas in India) but went upmarket when options available to backpackers weren't very nice (China, 1986).

What did we learn? It's the kind of obvious, yet profound, stuff most people learn on the road. First: People are different. The same information can be seen in incredibly different ways. Second: tolerance. We learned to tolerate those who don't see that information exactly as we do.

Traveling teaches you quickly to accept that things are not done as you are accustomed to them being done. It's a series of small lessons: Take off your shoes when entering the house in Japan and have yet another set of slippers for the loo, or walk with your elbows up in the crowds of Hong Kong. Learn these lessons and you'll be tolerant of differences for the rest of your life.

Travel teaches you that people might not react the way you think they should, so you need to be prepared for that. That's a simple but great management lesson.

CHAPTER 2

MY FUTURES PAST

Cut to: Chicago. I've just returned to the US from an overseas jaunt that involved McDonald's, grapefruit picking, and backpacking with my girlfriend. And I need a job. I'm a journalist in a world where positions are scarce and applicants plentiful. Jimmy Carter is president and I'm a member of a very unexclusive club: the unemployed!

To give me something to do and a bit of pocket money, my father helps me get a job as a runner on the floor of the Chicago Mercantile Exchange (CME), the "Merc." This was when the legendarily raucous trading pits were booming, long before the advent of electronic trading.

Runners wore yellow jackets, which identified us as the lowest of the low. The phone people would take a call, write out the order and hold the order in the air. The runner would grab the paper, take it quickly to the appropriate trading pit, and give it to our representative in that pit, who would give it to a trader to be fulfilled. If it was a "market" order it would be done in seconds. The trader would scribble the transaction price on the paper, which would then come back to the runner and the runner would take it back as quickly as possible to the phone person. That was my job. Four years at uni for this!

But it was a fascinating place: plenty of action and really high stakes—there was a lot of money in futures trading! One joke was about a trader having a tough day and muttering that he might not be able to make the payments on his Mercedes. The old-timer next to him in the pit says, "If you can't pay cash for your Mercedes then you shouldn't be here." I was a runner for a couple of months and only got promoted when I told my boss that I wasn't just there for summer holidays—this was actually my full-time job!

Next I was on the phones. I became the one who handed the orders to the runners! But the firm was changing. Futures trading had recently been deregulated. This meant that rather than charging a minimum commission for every trade, firms could charge what they liked.

This had happened in the stock market a few years earlier. A new industry was forming: discount trading, where consumers made their own choices and completed trades at a fraction of the old commission cost. Discount stock-trading firms were springing up everywhere, like Charles Schwab, one of the few still around today.

Futures trading had always been the unloved cousin of stock trading, and there was no surge of firms offering discounted futures trading. One of the top people at the firm I was with was a wacky older guy called Herb, who thought discounting could be an interesting business to get into. We were among the first to offer it, and I just happened to be there. We quickly became the biggest in the market.

HISTORY

The company, one of the bigger clearing houses on the CME, was run by Barry, a relatively young guy who was a futures trader. Herb was his uncle by marriage (i.e. not a blood relative; an important detail) who was trading for his own account from the company's offices.

Herb was quite a guy. He was about 60 when I joined the firm and had done just about everything: shrimp boat fisherman, real estate baron, wholesale meat company owner (that's the connection with my father). He'd tell stories of Chicago corruption, when he worked for "the world's richest policeman," rolling his eyes.

I joined the firm as a runner just as Herb was setting up a discount futures brokerage firm. After my stint as a runner, and then on the phones on the floor, I moved into the new part of the company: the discount brokerage. I started in the operations center, taking orders from customers, passing them down to the phone people on the exchange floor, and then calling the customers back to tell them of their filled orders.

Herb liked me and took me under his wing. We worked together for more than five years. I went from being on the phones with customers to joining the sales team, to joining the marketing team, to running the sales and marketing teams. I did that all in the space of 15 months. When I left the company after six years I was a senior vice president. I was 28 years old.

The first Christmas I was there we had about $5 million in customer funds. When I left, we had over $250 million in customer funds. And we were quite profitable.

As the company grew, so did I. Remember, I was a recent university graduate with no real business experience entering a world I knew nothing about. I recall vividly the first time Herb asked me to join a couple of visitors for lunch at a restaurant.

Normally, I either brought a sandwich to eat at my desk or grabbed some fast food. This was exciting!

As I looked over the menu—no $1.50 Big Macs here—I wondered if I'd be paying for my own lunch. I wasn't sure I had enough money in my wallet. I didn't dare ask, so I just ordered something simple (and cheap) and waited. Herb paid for everyone and I wiped the sweat from my brow.

I learned tons from Herb, sometimes by trying to imitate what he did and sometimes swearing I'd never do it the way he did it!

The Herb and Barry show

Sales and marketing was the engine room of the company. We advertised for business, brought it in, and did what we could to make sure it didn't leave. Our typical customer had time and disposable income—people like airline pilots and doctors. They wanted to trade futures on their own and, like a trip to Las Vegas, every once in a while they'd win, which kept them coming back. But, overall, they usually lost.

Herb made office life exciting. He was an idea machine and he encouraged others to feed his machine. We'd kick around this idea or that—for example, would it be easier to close a sale if we offered the person the first trade for free? I'd ask the salespeople, gather what figures I could, or we'd just have a few salespeople test an idea. This was great fun. A new industry with new ideas. We did everything ourselves, including advertising. Herb didn't believe in ad agencies. We wrote our own TV spots, hired crews to shoot them, sat with the director to edit them, and saw them on the air 10 days later. What a rush! Print ads were the same, as were deals with other companies—nothing off limits, and much of it was up to me to make happen.

Herb would come in each morning and walk around the office,

talking with everyone. He loved to flirt with the ladies, young or old. (This was 1982, remember.) He had a natural way of making people feel important and that their ideas were interesting. He'd also sound them out about his latest schemes and deals.

Herb loved change, but this proved a double-edged sword. The staff loved their interaction with him, how he put them at the front of what the company was doing. But after a while they tired of the incessant changes. What I saw was that they loved being entertained each day, but they didn't really want to have a different workplace from one day to the next; some stability was appreciated.

It reached the point where some employees would cringe when they saw Herb making his rounds. They knew he'd be asking them to do something differently, but they just wanted to get on with their jobs.

Herb also gave me lessons in negotiation. We would go into meetings with all the senior execs, maybe five or six of us, sitting in front of Barry, who was the president of the firm and sort of Herb's boss (as much as anyone could be Herb's boss). Barry sat at a big desk in a lavish office. More about this in a minute.

We'd be talking about how the advertising was doing. We spent a lot of money back then advertising in the *Wall Street Journal*, which was the daily bible for futures traders. And after a lot of discussion Herb would choose his moment: "I think we should cut out all the advertising. It's all wasted." Boom. The room was silent. Was this guy mad? So, Herb would repeat it. More silence. Then everyone would kind of speak up—how crazy that would be, how would we get any new business, etc. In the end, we'd agree to cut $50k or $100k from the monthly budget.

It took me a while to see the method behind his seeming madness. Herb never really wanted to cut out all the advertising. He just wanted us to focus on spending the money more wisely. He knew that if he could cut the budget we'd have to make the remaining money work even harder. He got exactly what he wanted.

In my six years there, I watched Herb's personality become more erratic. He had periods where he was clearly depressed. His powerful, positive effervescence would turn negative, bringing everyone around him down with a crash. It showed me how strong the influence of the leader was on those around her or him. This is an incredibly important point: You have a big influence on the people you manage. Herb could bring people down just as easily as he could bring them up. Maybe even more easily.

Herb and Barry agreed on nothing. They were truly chalk and cheese. The gap between uncle and nephew (by marriage, remember) was as wide as any you'd want to see on a management team. Sometimes this helped us reach good decisions and compromises. But not always!

Barry was a rich futures trader. Herb was an entrepreneurial genius. Herb wanted us to be in cheap offices to send the message that every penny spent was a penny less to grow the business with. Barry loved his giant dark-wood desk, which didn't even look that big in his vast office.

At one point we moved into a new building. We went from nice offices to plush. Barry called in an interior designer; Herb saw his fee and had a fit. Around that time Herb received a package that included an oddly shaped piece of Styrofoam. Herb, ever the prankster, put the Styrofoam on his wall. The interior decorator took a look at it and said it was a great piece of art—unusual, but he really liked it! Herb had a great laugh.

As for Barry, my best management lessons from him were in the "what not to do" category. They're no less valuable than positive lessons, but they can be more painful when you're going through them!

Take, for instance, our regular senior management meetings, where six or seven well-paid executives would decide the direction of the business. We'd be deep in conversation and Barry's phone (on that big desk) would ring. Barry would answer it. "OK. No. OK. Yes, three o'clock. Yes. Joe and Bob. Maybe Bill. What's wrong with George? All right then, three-thirty…" He'd hang up and turn back to us. The meeting, which had come to a complete stop, slowly restarted. Five minutes would go by and the phone would ring again. Same conversation. Same break in our meeting.

This was Barry arranging that afternoon's golf game! I would sit there during these stoppages and try to calculate the cost of all those executives doing nothing. And I'd look around at all the bored faces, some people doodling on their note-pads, perhaps a couple of people conversing quietly. What a message to send to your most senior executives: "You are unimportant compared to my golf arrangements."

I never understood this behavior. Were we not united in a common goal of making our company successful? Shouldn't we all be rowing really hard in the same direction? Or was this company just Barry's toy, for him to play with when and how he wanted? That's how it felt.

Here's another lesson-in-reverse from Barry that I'll come back to often: Remember how important you are to the people you manage.

One day I passed a young woman in the corridor who was in tears. I hesitated, but had to ask, "What's the matter?" Between sniffles, she said, "I just passed the boss in the hall. I said good morning to him and he didn't say anything back. I'm sure I'm about to be fired."

I'm certain that if I had gone to Barry at that precise moment and asked him why he ignored her, he'd say, "What girl?" I'll bet he never even saw her. He was probably coming up from the trading pit and reviewing a stack of cards marked up with all his trades.

He forgot how important he was to the people he managed. She was in tears, and he didn't know she existed. Bad story. Great learning.

Through the years I've constantly reminded myself that, as a manager, I'm always on stage. People will react to what you say or do far more than you think it deserves. One time a colleague and I went to visit another business. I always find it interesting to visit businesses that aren't in your industry because they usually have similar problems and often have very different ways of approaching them.

This was a very different business to car insurance but still involved managing and motivating people. The leader of the business had taken over a few years before and done great things with it. Before he arrived it was scruffy, to say the least. He got the team focused on the mission and did a lot to encourage and motivate people. Soon they were being recognized on lists of Best Companies to Work For in their area.

The leader is a very good guy—funny, with a very dry, often biting, sense of humor. As he's showing us around, one of his senior managers arrives—a nice woman wearing quite a novel outfit. He introduces us to her and we exchange pleasantries. As we're getting ready to resume our tour, he looks at her and says, "Well, I see it's pajama day in the finance department, eh?"

She looks like a deer in the headlights. She stammers a bit and says, "Uh, actually everyone's wearing this these days." The CEO chuckles, doesn't think twice about it, and continues our tour.

So, a senior executive has been told by the head of the company, in front of guests, that it looks like she's wearing pajamas. I can guarantee you one thing: She will <u>never</u> wear that outfit to the office again. Maybe never wear it again, full stop.

The CEO simply forgot how important he was to the people he managed. He thought he was being clever, but he forgot how this might come across to her. Maybe if we hadn't been there she might have laughed it off. But to be introduced like that to people—guests of the CEO, no less—is a classic example of management inattention. You are incredibly important to the people you manage—something I cannot repeat often enough. The problem is, even good managers, like this CEO, sometimes forget.

As a great manager, you must constantly remind yourself how important you are to those people you manage. In the instance when you do forget, and these instances will definitely happen, go back and explain or apologize. Your people will understand; they know even super managers are human. To humbly say, "Whoops, I dropped the ball on that one," is a sign of strength, not weakness.

Just recently a talented member of the team, let's call her Bobbi, was telling me that she had finished a major project and that she'd been promised a certain role going forward. But then a new team member was added, and in a team meeting the boss essentially gave the new person the very duties that had been promised to Bobbi.

Bobbi was clearly stressed as she explained the situation to me. She said if she didn't get clarification, she was certain to lose a night's sleep. She hadn't spoken up at the meeting because she wondered if she had done something wrong, or perhaps her manager wasn't happy with her work.

Now I knew the boss in question, so I was sure that it was

a misunderstanding or oversight. Maybe the boss had forgotten the commitment she'd made, or the new team member's job was actually different. Whatever the explanation, one thing was clear: The boss forgot how important she was to the people she managed. This boss had a million things going on. This was just one of them. It was understandable. But it didn't have to happen.

The discussion of Bobbi's new role had probably been forgotten, parked in the back of the boss's memory garage. Of course, to Bobbi this was the most important conversation of the month or even year! The boss may have spontaneously tossed the new team member something interesting, trying to make him or her feel welcome, forgetting she'd promised it to someone else. The situation did get cleared up quickly. The boss was extremely approachable, and Bobbi was assured that she'd done nothing wrong and would still have the duties promised, and that what was on offer to the new member of the team was a bit different. Bobbi slept well that night.

Dos and don'ts from Herb and Barry

DO
✓ Keep the office energized and interesting.
✓ Start negotiations at an extreme position.
✓ Encourage creativity.
✓ Realize that your attitude affects the whole staff.
✓ Remember how important you are to people you manage.

DON'T
✓ Use the company as your toy.
✓ Change things so frequently that people can't keep up.
✓ Be so focused that you don't see the people around you.

CHAPTER 3

FRENCH LESSONS

In the six years I spent in Chicago in the discount futures trading business, I worked in operations, sales, sales management, marketing and advertising, made a few deals with suppliers, and even opened a European office. (I also married my girlfriend!) In my last year in the futures business, I served as the taffy in a taffy-pull between Herb and Barry. It was not comfortable and didn't end well. But I got a handsome payout, largely because Herb appreciated all I'd done early on.

That's another lesson I'll return to: Don't forget how others helped put you where you are today. Admiral, a multi-billion-pound company that more than 10,000 people work for today, rests on the foundation built by a small group of people more than a quarter of a century ago. Specifically, January 2, 1993.

At Admiral, I instituted a tradition of all Day 1 staff who are still with the company getting together for tea, coffee and biscuits early in the new year. I started this after our first year and it's happened every year since. Of course, as people have left the company there have been fewer and fewer participants each time. There has always been a small gift, some of which are laughable now (who can forget those £4 watches?). We sit around for an hour or so and remember the old days and all the characters we've worked with over the years. It's very nice for the people who are still around to be singled out for this cup of tea. We even did this via Zoom in Covid times.

Never forget the people who built the foundation upon which your company now sits. You have them to thank.

But back to the 1980s. Diane, my wife, and I were still in our twenties and ready for an adventure: backpacking through Asia. As you'd expect, we saw incredible sights and met amazing people and were struck by their generosity and hospitality. So many people we met had very little but were happy to share what they had with us.

We saw big changes happening. In China, we didn't have to register with the local police in every new city—a year earlier, we would have. We saw the ancient past, like the Great Wall, and age-old practices still being used, like people building roads by hand—literally shaping bricks and laying them one by one into position. Or individuals pulling big carts full of bricks, dirt, wood, or vegetables.

We learned (the hard way) to be precise in communicating. Leaving China, we were ready for a bit of comfort, so we looked for a cruise ship to take us from Shanghai to Hong Kong. We found one and asked if it had a pool. Yes! was the answer. We booked it, looking forward to some sunning and swimming. After we settled in our cabin, we went looking for the pool. We found it. It was true, the ship had a pool. But there was no water in it.

At one point, we stopped in Singapore to recharge our batteries (metaphorically—no cell phones or iPads back then). We found Singapore to be a bit of Zurich in the middle of Asia. We could drink the water from the tap! Eat the meat! Paradise! We also started to think: what next? I wasn't keen to go back into futures, but I realized that if I switched to another industry I was going to have to start close to the bottom. I wanted to find a place other than futures where I got credit for my experience. Diane and I thought maybe getting a Master's in Business Administration degree (MBA) would be a good move for me—I could learn other aspects of business and possibly go into another industry without starting at the bottom. Diane was a lawyer in both France and the US, so she could get a job practically anywhere. That made our decision easier.

I had seen an article in a French magazine a few years earlier about an international business school outside Paris. It showed photos of young people sitting in groups on the lawn, in the sunshine, discussing the business issues of the day. It was called INSEAD—a French acronym for Institut Européen d'Administration des Affaires (or European Institute of Business Administration).

I visited the American embassy in Singapore to find out more. Besides the green lawn and international student body, there were two other big advantages of enrolling at INSEAD. It was only a one-year program, not two as in American business schools. That meant only one year with no income, not two. And the average age of the student body was almost 30. I was 28 sitting in the embassy in Singapore and would be 29 by the time I could start any MBA program. Most of the students in US programs were a lot younger.

When we got back to France in January, we visited INSEAD, in Fontainebleau. It's just 60km from Paris, but it took us four grueling hours to drive there in a snowstorm they still talk about. But it looked good and quickly became our first choice of MBA program. In the February, I took the GMAT aptitude test and applied to INSEAD and a couple of US schools. I got accepted at my undergraduate alma mater, Michigan, conditional on my taking (and presumably passing) an advanced mathematics course. Great!

I started the class at a university near Chicago. I hadn't taken math since high school, and it felt like I was being taught how to speak Martian. In the meantime INSEAD had lost my application, making me wait extra time. This was a nightmare. But—whew!— eventually INSEAD came through, offering me a place. To this day I don't think I would have passed that math class and so would have been rejected by Michigan. What then?

The MBA program was a real eye-opener. Classes were taught in English, but being back in school after a hiatus of nearly a decade was a shock to the system. The course was divided into five modules. The first two were required classes and Module 3 was a mix of required and elective classes. Modules 4 and 5 were all electives.

Not since the physical labor of being a beef lugger had I worked as hard as I did those first two modules. I would have class most of the day, get home, have dinner with Diane (if you've got to study a lot then do it in France where the dinner is always great, even if it's just cheese and bread!), then start my studying. I'd work until midnight, sleep, then get up at 6 am to study for an hour or two before class. This was the routine from September to December. In exam times I worked a bit harder!

On the very first day of class at INSEAD, in September 1987, I learned one of the best management lessons I ever had: The power of the team is invariably greater than the power of any single individual.

The lesson actually started before the first day. We picked up our books and also got our first assignment: the Canadian Arctic Survival Test. Intriguing, right? It's a short story about a small plane that crashes in the Canadian Arctic. There are 16 items salvaged from the plane. Your job is to rank the items in order of importance—e.g. is the bottle of water more important than the flashlight? We each did this on our own the night before our first class.

The next day, 172 MBA candidates, all keen as mustard and bright as buttons, were broken into 22 teams of seven or eight. Even that was clever: The optimum number for teamwork is supposedly four or five, but they were preparing us for the real world, where teams aren't always the ideal size. I'd also heard that the administrators went through our applications and tried to team up people they thought might not get on with each other. This, again, was to simulate the real world, where you don't always choose teammates and don't necessarily like everyone around you. Our team of eight was all male, from all over the world, meeting for the first time: one Lebanese, one Japanese, one Luxembourger, one Swede, one Austrian, one Frenchman, one Brit and me, the lone American. It was all friendly—at first, anyway.

A lot of good things came out of my INSEAD time. First and foremost was meeting and becoming friends with David Stevens. We did a couple of interesting projects together, and a few years later, as I was setting up Admiral, almost as a lark, I asked David if he'd like to join. Getting David to say "yes" to joining Admiral was probably the best single thing I ever did at the company, and that was 18 months before launch. Which means since then, my contribution to Admiral has been on a downhill slope!

We met around a small table in a workroom, debating the list and hammering out a consensus on the 16 items. Back in the big lecture amphitheater, everyone was told how the experts ranked the items. We graded our own personal lists and our team list against the experts.

So, 172 really bright individuals in 22 teams. How many individuals outperformed their team's score?

The answer was two. That meant 170 really talented MBA candidates, on their first day of school, trying their best to impress, did <u>not</u> outperform their team's score. A powerful first-day lesson: The power of the team is invariably greater than the power of virtually any single individual.

This lesson sticks with me today, more than 30 years later, which I've distilled into a simple, memorable phrase: The Team, the Team, the Team. (I borrowed the expression from a legendary football coach at Michigan, Bo Schembechler.)

It pays to seek other opinions before doing just about anything. In almost every instance, outside input will improve the quality of your decision-making. I will come back to this time and again in this training manual: The Team, the Team, the Team. The power of the team is greater than the power of the individual. On my last day as CEO at Admiral, I was surprised to see everyone wearing a T-shirt with my face on the front. I was not surprised that first on the list of "Henry-isms" printed on the back was "The Team, the Team, the Team." I guess it sank in.

Later in this book is a chapter on leadership and decision-making. What is the best tool for making great decisions? You talk with others, you work within teams, you realize that you don't need to be Superman/woman (that's yet another chapter later on!) to be a great manager.

By Christmas break at INSEAD we were done with the first

two compulsory modules, which were very hard. I worked my socks off. But I got a little taster of accounting, finance, statistics, organizational behavior, and so on. We also got a shocking real-world lesson: the stock market crash of October 1987. Overnight the banks stopped recruiting. One bank was on campus recruiting that week, and the recruiters were informed that their jobs had been made redundant—but please, they were told, complete the recruitment interviews. The recruiters did so, but they said they suspected it wouldn't be all that valuable to those interviewing.

The last three modules, from January to July, were marked by less work, the birth of our first child, and doing projects with David and another friend, Tim. I also performed a regression analysis for one class to try to determine what factors from our CVs got us on the interview lists submitted by the companies that came to recruit.

David, Tim and I worked together on two fascinating projects. The first was on finding links, if any, between perfume advertising and what was in the bottle. Perfume proved to be a bizarre world. Almost no one could identify perfumes from a blind smell test, but people did identify what kind of perfume it was from the advertising. The advertising was plentiful in French magazines and we studied various brands projecting images of luxury, calm, seduction, aggressiveness, and so on. Liquid in a bottle. Incredible.

The second project was even more fun, as we turned to a more appealing liquid: beer! Our project was to assess what a beer bottle says about the beer inside: long necks, short necks, green bottles, brown bottles. For instance, we found a normal-sized, metallic bottle with a stopper attached. What message is sent by a stopper in the bottle? That you wouldn't want to finish it. A regular-sized beer you wouldn't finish in one go?! What must be in there? We spent a few excellent afternoons in David's garden, testing beers—I mean, of course, testing what bottles meant to the beer. And the beer with a stopper was true to its unspoken message: It took the three of us to finish one, and we laughed the rest of the afternoon!

These projects—and case studies in class—were more than fun. It was a great way to gain insight, albeit briefly, into different industries and what was "normal" for those industries. A few years later we would transfer one industry's norm to the insurance industry, where it wasn't normal, with great success. Learning is everywhere.

The regression analysis I performed also proved interesting— and illuminating. When companies came to recruit at INSEAD, they would send out a list of the students they wanted to see. If you were on a list, you could choose whether or not to meet with that company. If you weren't on a list you could ask to be interviewed, but it'd be up to the company.

I wanted to see if I could determine what factors would get you on those interview lists. So I took all the basic info from the CV book—gender, age, nationality, languages spoken, education, prior work, etc.—and then married them to the names of the people on the lists sent in by the companies.

Only two things came up as statistically significant. Unfortunately, I only remember one, and with great clarity, for obvious reasons: North Americans didn't get interviews. Now maybe that was a reflection of the talent from the US, Canada, and Mexico. But there were quite a few of us, many intelligent and talented, so it seemed to be an element of the recruitment, not of the talent pool. I guess it made sense. European companies weren't really looking for North Americans to work in Europe, and North American companies recruited in North America, not Europe. Sadly, in my case, my analysis proved correct. I didn't get invited by any companies for an interview. So instead, I did the asking and some obliged. I got one job offer, from an American consulting firm that had an office in Croydon, south London. The man who recruited me, who became my boss, was American.

I wasn't all that keen on becoming a consultant, but I now had a young family, our savings were pretty much depleted and I had to get on with making a living. The UK was a good location for a Frenchwoman and a Yank. We'd lived in the US, where Diane wasn't hugely happy, and we'd lived in France, where I wasn't hugely happy. Now we were headed to neutral territory!

I learned quickly that I didn't like consulting. Perhaps it was the firm I was with, which wasn't the greatest. I was involved in bidding for a couple of contracts and the effort the managers exerted was always aimed at how we could extract the greatest amount of value for the least amount of work and still get the contract. One time, we bid for something to do with airplane leasing and our bid was five times more than the next! Whoops.

My boss was a good guy and, as he had a core client, he didn't bid on too many other projects. I did work on a couple of interesting projects for him but, as consultants, it seemed we were always on the periphery of the firms we worked for, not at the center. Before this job, my experience had always been in the "decide and do" mode. So just to do some research and maybe lob in an idea or two that I'd never hear about again did not suit me.

Remember how a magazine article led me to INSEAD? I read a lot because I know that learning can happen anywhere. So can opportunity. One day I was flipping through a marketing magazine when I saw a recruitment ad for a company that hadn't started yet, didn't have a name, was in direct response financial services, and was looking for a marketing manager. Was my old firm from Chicago setting up in the UK? I didn't think much about it until a week later when, reading a different marketing magazine, I was stopped by the same ad.

I thought: "Wow, if this has stopped me twice, I should do something about it." And I did.

Homework assignments

✓ Never forget the people who helped you in the past.

✓ Learn wherever you go.

✓ Imagine how customers may perceive your products.

✓ Read magazines.

CHAPTER 4

INSURANCE? AMAZING!

The advertisement had only said "Financial services." When I called to set up the interview, I asked the woman, "What financial service is it, exactly?" She sounded embarrassed as she meekly replied, "Car insurance." I took the phone from my ear, looked at it and thought, "Oh no. What could be more boring than car insurance?"

But I really didn't like being a management consultant. So I went for the job, got it, and became the first marketing and sales manager for what became Churchill Insurance.

What I quickly found out was that car insurance is an amazing business. And in 1988, it was changing rapidly, from face-to-face sales to telephone sales. Pricing was complex and fascinating

(how many products have a different price for every customer?).
Advertising was great fun, managing a sales department was a
brilliant experience, computers were making incredible things
possible—and it was a ginormous industry!

Here's a lesson I learned: When you get into something, any
business is fascinating. Somebody out there is making buttons
and getting very excited because they're coming out with a new
five-holer—and it's going to be green! I'm not mocking—I admire
that. Business is just interesting. If you don't agree, you may be in
the wrong field (and I'm wondering how you got hired).

I loved the challenges I now faced. Understanding why people
do things the way they do and how you can influence them to do
things differently. How to deal with customers, staff, suppliers.
Being creative so your product can give value to both customer
and shareholder alike. And leading people to make it happen.
It's all amazing. If you don't have a passion for business—and
for learning about business—it's going to be tough to be a great
manager.

So out of the consulting world and into a start-up I went. I
joined Churchill in November 1988 and we launched on June
19, 1989. Churchill was one of the first car insurers in the UK to
cut out the middleman—we'd transact directly with customers,
everything over the phone. We had only one office when we
launched, with some 70 staff.

Later I made sure that Admiral was an egalitarian company,
long before it became fashionable—no company cars, no company
dining room, same desk and chair for all. This all stemmed from
my experiences at Churchill. Because that's not the way they did
it there.

Here's a story about not keeping promises. When I joined
Churchill, I negotiated a bonus of £5,000 in my contract for

launching on schedule. The launch date, already decided when I arrived, was seared into our minds: June 19, 1989. Nothing was going to stand in our way. The managing director said he would not accept anything later. OK, that's fair enough.

Those first two difficult modules at INSEAD were great preparation for the pre-launch work at Churchill. My assistant and I worked every day during April and took but one day off in May. Sixty working days out of 61 days. We were setting up all the communication with customers and the newspaper adverts—by hand on our new Macintosh computer. Often we'd work until 2 or 3 am and be back in the office before 10 am the next day. We designed and created all the letters and brochures customers would receive. Some of it can now be done in minutes, but we didn't have the option to wait 30 years to make it easy on ourselves—we had a June 19 launch date to hit.

I was fortunate—a lot of the things I'd done in Chicago paid off big time in the UK. Some of them became commonplace, like a Freephone number for sales (already the norm in the US, but Churchill was one of the first, if not the first, to do this in the UK).

Come June 19, we launched, right on time. The marketing was all there. The adverts were running. The phone rang, the sales force fielded the calls and sold policies. The IT worked most of the time, though it was far from perfect. (The system wasn't quite ready to print policy documents. In those first days, my marketing assistant and our HR manager had to print the documents by hand, so to speak: inputting names and addresses of each customer, and printing it all on our office printer.)

We were off! But no bonus. I soon found out that a number of other senior managers also hadn't received promised bonuses. In July, one of the managers had a chat with the MD about it. The

INSURANCE? AMAZING!

At Churchill, we designed an A4 brochure to go out with the policy documents, similar to what I'd created in the futures discount brokerage firm. The brochure had pictures of the staff at work, some reassuring copy, and a bit about our owner, a big Swiss insurer.

There was a pocket at the back where we put all the policy docs: schedule, certificate, etc.

We got rave reviews from customers for this brochure—it was unheard of in UK personal lines insurance at the time. Our competitors sent a small envelope where documents spilled out randomly when you opened it and you were left with a pile of folded documents. There were no warm words about the company.

Why did customers love the brochure? They told us it wasn't really the words reassuring them that they had bought their car insurance from a reputable supplier. It was that pocket in the back, where they could store their documents. They could just take the brochure and put it in a cabinet or drawer and not think about it again. Live and learn.

MD's explanation: Because the IT wasn't perfect, he wasn't sure it was truly a timely launch.

What?! Are you joking? I'd worked my socks off to hit that launch date, and we started selling policies that very day and never stopped. That's timely! In August, I went to see the MD to demand my bonus, feeling dirty. But I had worked damned hard and was going to fight to get what I was owed. Grudgingly the MD said, OK, the bonus would be in my next month's pay.

This was just one of the many things the guy had done to make me concerned. The delayed bonus was a key moment of realization that this was not going to be my long-term home. I could feel what little loyalty I had draining out. Imagine, however, if the MD had come up to me on June 19 and said, "Henry, great job—the marketing looks great, the adverts are running and we're selling policies," shook my hand and gave me a check for £5,000. He would not only have given me a proper reward but he would have earned my loyalty.

But the way he went about it, this bonus actually made me disloyal. There was a delicious karmic consequence to his behavior, though. That disloyalty eventually led to the creation of a competitor, which outshone Churchill at every turn. (I think you know who that is.)

The moral of the story: When you give someone a reward, do it right. Congratulate them. It's simple. Never say, "Here's the reward but…" Just say, "Here's the reward; great job!" If you're going to spend the money on the reward you might as well reap the benefit of the good feeling and loyalty it should engender. In my case, the MD could have spent the £5,000 and made me a happy camper. Not only didn't it come out as a reward, it was demeaning to make me ask. It was a negative incentive! How silly is that? He gained nothing… and it still cost him the £5,000! After a bit more than two years at Churchill I got a call one day from a headhunter. Somebody was planning to set up a direct car insurance operation and was looking for a managing director; would I be interested? Little did they know that they could have offered me a pay cut and I would have leapt at the chance. There was so much wrong at Churchill, and it came straight from the top. It was a toxic atmosphere and I had lost all my enthusiasm by then. When the headhunter came calling, I was definitely answering the phone.

I officially joined what became Admiral at the end of June 1991. The parent company gave me my IT director. I recruited a woman who was a smart market research consultant who'd impressed me with work she'd done for Churchill. I then was fortunate to recruit David and, lastly, another woman who had worked for me in the marketing department at Churchill.

The five of us went to work in that small office on a business plan—our business plan. My enthusiasm flooded back. As the guy in charge, I could put all the negative lessons I'd learned throughout my career to use by doing the opposite. Working on something new in close quarters like that energized us all. Ideas flew, and maybe some sparks. It wasn't long after launch that the smart market research consultant and David were married.

Churchillian inspiration

✓ Only dull people get bored.
✓ Any business can be fascinating.
✓ Live up to your promises.
✓ Express appreciation.

CHAPTER 5

THE START OF
SOMETHING BIG

When you look at the graphs showing Admiral's growth and profits you might imagine that its history has been one long, lovely yellow brick road.

Ha! Nothing could be further from the truth. We fought horrible battles in the early years, with the parent company and with some of the senior managers. On numerous evenings in those first five years, I went home thinking I had just spent my last day at Admiral—I was either going to quit or get sacked. At one point, after a visit from the parent company, we had to have our office swept for bugs. And I'm not referring to the creepy-crawly kind.

This is a training manual, not a history book, so I'll try not to dwell on the past. But those early years are interesting, and so out of sync with the rest of our history that they reveal valuable lessons.

It all starts with the parent company. When I got the call from the search firm, I was the marketing and sales manager at Churchill. It was clear that all the big insurers and a number of other organizations were looking at selling car insurance direct to the public rather than via intermediaries. I was quite keen to find out who might be out there doing a search. I was a bit perplexed when I was told it was a managing agent at Lloyd's of London called Hayter Brockbank (later renamed the Brockbank Group).

What in the world, I wondered, was a "managing agent at Lloyd's of London"?

I learned that the Lloyd's structure was similar to what I'd grown up with at the Chicago Mercantile Exchange. Lloyd's, like the CME, is just a place. The CME had traders in the pit, while Lloyd's had underwriters who wrote insurance risks. Underwriters were grouped into syndicates and worked under a managing agent.

Alongside the managing agent were member agents, who found and distributed the money—the capital behind it all. The people providing the capital were called "Names." They were generally rich people, including many whose assets weren't liquid—like a stately manor or fancy paintings. By pledging these assets to Lloyd's they'd get credit for providing capital, so those assets that just sat there started generating a return. The Names invested in syndicates who put their capital to use to underwrite insurance risks. Syndicates were managed by managing agents. Simply put, member agents raised the capital, managing agents put it to work.

One cheeky thing I did before I was hired was key to the future of Admiral. When I was negotiating my terms, I asked for an equity stake in the business for me and my management team. This was the going thing at the time; the MD at Churchill had persuaded Churchill's Swiss parent to give him equity. "Why not ask," I thought? "What's the worst they could say?"

So, I took my shot. Lloyd's was unlike a typical big, corporate insurance company—ownership, profit commissions and the like were quite the norm. I almost randomly picked a number and asked for 25 percent equity for me and my management team. I was kind of shocked when they said... "OK." Really?

My team and I would own a quarter of this new venture. Suddenly writing a business plan became a lot more interesting. (A few months into writing the plan, Mark and George, the underwriting and back office heads of the firm respectively, called us in to discuss that 25 percent. They gently told us they were going back on their promise. Gulp. We waited. They said they thought the right number was—we were holding our breath—20 percent. Ah. Not 25 percent but 20 percent. Ahhhh. We looked pained, pointed to the original deal, but realized compromise was required. We were business people, right? So, yes, we could see their point of view. OK, fine, we magnanimously agreed to the reduction. And we did cartwheels in the street all the way back to our office!)

I parceled out equity as soon as I had it. The other four original starters all got 2 percent. The next wave of managers got 1 percent each and the third wave got half a percentage point each. In all, I distributed 12 percent of the 20 percent and was planning further distributions when the shit hit the proverbial fan.

I officially joined in June 1991, with a planned launch date of January 2, 1993. The original team was five. I was assigned my IT manager, Dave, who was a friend of Mark, the underwriter. (IT Dave is not to be confused with David Stevens.)

To say that IT Dave was a complicated personality is like saying the sun is hot. IT Dave came from a company that had been bought out by IBM. So he was kind of an IBM guy, always wearing a white shirt and tie to the office. I'm told that every January 2 he would go out to the sales and buy five white shirts: Monday, Tuesday, Wednesday, Thursday, and Friday. And he would throw last year's shirts away.

My first recruit, Heather, the woman who worked for the market research consultancy I'd engaged when I was with Churchill, had mentioned that she was planning to move to Perth, Australia, so I didn't expect her to say yes. But she changed her mind and accepted the offer! Great! She was a jack of all trades. She did research, facilities, marketing, planning, strategy, logistics, recruiting and more in her time.

Next, I contacted David, my classmate from INSEAD. He'd landed a job in London at McKinsey, the prestigious management consultancy. We'd meet socially from time to time after INSEAD. His opinion of McKinsey went from "Great" to "OK" to a bit of grumbling. I almost apologetically asked him if he wanted to join this car insurance startup, and I was stunned when he didn't say no, but said "Maybe." Wow! It took quite a bit to convince him, but Heather and I were able to charm him into it. OK, maybe it was mostly Heather. They married shortly after launch, have three children and have been together some 30 years and counting!

The last member of the team was a lady who was in my marketing department at Churchill. Unfortunately, when we moved to Cardiff, she was unable to relocate with us and so, after a year of commuting from the south-east to Cardiff, she left the company.

What was this business going to be? At first, the plan was for pan-European direct-response car insurance. We even took a field trip to France to explore that market, and David went on to study the German market. As we started to put together the pan-European plan, however, we realized that it might just be prudent to prove ourselves capable in the UK before trying to dominate Europe! In the end, the plan we presented to the board was for the UK only. We stayed that way for 15 years until we finally moved forward with that original plan and launched an operation in Spain.

There we were: a tight team of five. Mostly. What I hadn't reckoned on was that IT Dave didn't like me very much. One tip-off was when he introduced me to a supplier as the marketing manager, not the managing director! (Afterwards, I asked him why and he stammered a bit, saying he thought having the MD in tow would have seemed heavy-handed. Right.)

This was made worse when, early in 1992, we had to find an underwriter—someone to price the policies and determine the criteria for which we would even offer a policy. I was a bit naïve and didn't yet know that at Lloyd's underwriters were king. Managing directors were not. We struggled to find an underwriter. We were looking for someone strong in statistics, data analysis, math, who had a good grip on the entire business. Turns out we were ahead of our time.

Back then all the people we interviewed had basically gotten into the insurance industry either before A levels or just after. I don't remember if any of them had university degrees. They had worked in a variety of areas of insurance, stepping on toes and shoulders on their way up. By the time they reached the age of 35 or 40, they were underwriters or in other senior positions.

That's when we came up with the idea to split this job. We'd create a Pricing department that would set the prices while the Underwriting department would be responsible for the rules. This was revolutionary in its day. Or should I say heresy?!

But Lloyd's wasn't ready for revolution. The people in the

parent company looked at us as if we had fallen on our heads. You could not operate with just statisticians and math whizzes, they told us—you had to have a face of the syndicate and that face was the underwriter. We were becoming stressed. The rates needed to be plugged into the IT system soon if we were going to make our January 1993 launch date. And we also needed an underwriter to be the signatory for our policies. Pressed by time, we made a bad hiring decision. We hired a traditional car insurance underwriter.

Painful lesson learned: The worst recruitments are those done when pressed by time. (More on that later.)

Here's an example of the way things were going. We were going to relocate the business from London to Cardiff and, of course, wanted to make sure those of us moving wouldn't be out of pocket. The property market had just crashed and two of us would have to sell our homes, myself and the underwriter, and this was clearly going to be at a loss. When I discussed the relocation packages with Mark, he simply said, "That's fine for the underwriter but no one else."

Hunh? I almost quit right then and there. Fortunately, George got involved and confirmed that the managing director would get the package as well.

A lot of this book is about building good teams and about senior managers working closely together. On January 2, 1993 we were about as far away from that utopia as imaginable. There were about four managers, including IT Dave and the underwriter on one side, and four, including myself, David, Heather and our finance director, Andrew, on the other side. And then there were a bunch of managers caught in the middle! It was a management team seemingly intent on snatching defeat from the jaws of victory!

The stress in the company was terrible. I was a walker—still am—and would try to walk all four floors of our building several times a day to talk with people—56 employees at the time—to see how things were going. The underwriter sat on one floor with the Underwriting and Customer Service teams. As time went on, I found the temperature on this floor getting colder and colder. I had to summon my courage up each time I went to this floor to do my walkabout. I could feel the underwriter shooting daggers in my back as I walked around.

Despite the tension and dysfunctionality of the management team, the business went brilliantly. We were lucky to launch when we did: 1993 was God's gift to car insurers, especially those with no history to worry about. Prices had started going up in 1992, soared in 1993, and continued to rise into 1994. Rising prices mean people shop around more, which played in our favor. Moreover, the existing insurers were putting prices up beyond the burn cost of the risk at that moment to make up some of the losses of previous years. We had no previous years, so no losses to make up. So, we priced for the cost of the day, which was often lower than the competition.

But our successful start was not merely down to luck. We had made a decision in creating the business plan that defined the success of Admiral. The decision: choosing a target market that appeared risky. This choice paid dividends early on and continues to pay dividends today.

We went totally against conventional wisdom and chose to target people who paid higher premiums. Obvious strategy—go where the money is, right? Not at all. The premiums were higher because the risk was higher.

It bears reminding that we were the seventh direct-response firm to enter the market. This surprises many people who assume we were first or second, and that we rode a first-mover advantage to success. Sorry, that wasn't the case. The first one had started almost a decade earlier. The leader in the direct market at that time, Direct Line, was second and was already five or six years old when we launched.

We reasoned that on Day 1 we were not going to have an economic advantage against the direct response firms that started ahead of us. But we saw that those other six firms were all fishing in the same pond: good drivers. They were all targeting drivers over 40, with smaller cars, who lived outside city centers. Their target customers paid premiums a little below the average of the entire market.

If we couldn't compete with the direct firms, then who could we compete with? Well, direct response was still nascent at this stage: less than 15 percent of the market. Everyone else went through intermediaries, mostly brokers. In the UK at the time, the broker's commission was roughly 15 percent a year.

My ultimate wish list

When we started Admiral, I wanted it to be a better place to work than Churchill had been—or any of the companies where I'd worked. I turned that vague aspiration into a more focused list of things that I wanted in our new company.

I asked everyone on the original team to do the same. For 25 years we asked every new Admiral employee to make their own list. I read every one—for the first decade, anyway. The lists obviously helped inform those of us in leadership. But they also helped new employees realize that they have input and a bit of control over their new workplace. Ideally, managers would review the employees' forms after a year. Not sure many did.

But we can review my original list, three decades later! I think we've done pretty well. Here's what I wrote in June 1991:

I want to work for a company...

1. That always treats customers, employees, and vendors with respect and dignity.
2. Where everyone in the company cares for the company as if it is his/her own company.
3. Where good people are rewarded; where hard work is rewarded; where good work is rewarded.
4. Where good ideas come from people at all levels of the company.
5. That treats individuals as individuals, be they customers, employees, or vendors.
6. Where the company bends over backwards to help employees who bend over backwards to help the company.
7. That is proud to sell its products and services to customers.
8. That works hard every day to satisfy the demands of customers.
9. Where people work together for a common goal.

We did the math. If a customer with a broker paid £500, the broker would get £75 and the insurer would keep £425. The broker would get this commission every year, even if the customer stayed with the same insurer. That meant that over five years the customer would pay £2,500, the broker would get £375 and the insurer would get £2,125.

The way we looked at it, because we would "own" the customer without an intermediary, we'd have an economic advantage if we could acquire the customer for less than £375 and keep the customer for five years.

We pushed this logic further: If we could acquire the customer for less than £75 then we wouldn't have to wait five years to have an economic advantage. It would be immediate!

We could then apply this advantage to the customer's rate. If we could acquire the customer for £50 then we could charge £490, saving the customer £10, and we would have £440 left to cover claims and expenses, which is £15 more than the broker-insurer would have.

The customer saves money *and* we have more margin. Sweet!

As you can see from this example, the higher the premium, the more we would have available to spend on acquisition and still hold an advantage. If a customer was only paying £250, then the broker's commission was only £37.50, and that's what we'd have to compete against.

The key was that direct marketing costs were not correlated with premium. In fact, it might be argued that it was just the opposite.

The customers with higher average premiums were generally younger city dwellers and/or drivers of larger, more expensive cars. This, it turned out, was a much-underserved part of the market, and so there was a bonus opportunity: These consumers responded very well to targeted advertising.

Most insurers ran away from these drivers, leery of the volatile claims result. At Churchill, the CEO decided to stop quoting for drivers under the age of 25 because he was so afraid of the potential underwriting result. He wasn't alone. When other companies stopped quoting for these customers that just meant less competition in our chosen segment, and less competition implies greater margin potential. These other companies weren't quoting or writing even a little bit of that business, so they had no data. In all things, from understanding markets to running an office, it helps to do a little bit of everything as education, if for no other reason. A little bit of knowledge is like a torch in a dark room: It's likely to be enough to find the door!

Moreover, the higher the premium the more likely a consumer was to shop around to get the best price because they were likely to save substantial money. It makes sense. How much can someone paying a £250 premium save? But someone paying £500 or £750 could save a lot of money.

So, we targeted "higher-premium customers," but not the extreme part of the market. The extreme part of the market is small but also even more volatile than our segment. Our average premium in those early years was probably some 35 to 50 percent higher than the market average. We'd run advertisements that spoke directly to our defined segment: "Are you paying over £400 for your car insurance?"

This targeting strategy worked a treat. We quickly found that our acquisition costs were actually *lower* than I had achieved at Churchill when targeting "good" drivers—and the premiums were much higher! The cost to service these customers was greater than the cost to service "good" drivers. Higher-premium/higher-risk drivers made more claims for one thing, which cost money to service. However, that increase in servicing cost was less than the overall increase in premium.

In insurance you separate the costs of your business in two

parts: the loss ratio, which is the cost of the claims divided by the premium income, and the expense ratio, which is all your other costs divided by the premium income. These ratios are calculated separately and then added together and called, wait for it… the "combined ratio." Admiral has, for most of its existence, been a leader in having the lowest expense ratio in the market. This is, in part, because we're pretty efficient but it's also because this is a ratio and our income was higher per client.

On the loss ratio side, we were able to create a big advantage versus the competition. After a couple of difficult years we did part company with the underwriter and David took over this area. Once he took over the pricing Admiral showed that this segment could produce market-leading loss ratios. For the better part of two decades, in what is assumed to be a commodity-like market, we had combined ratios 10 to 25 percentage points better than the market average. Stunning.

On the pricing side we did many things to create this advantage but here's a simple illustration of one thing we did: We asked more questions than our competitors.

This might sound counter-productive because asking more questions meant taking more of the customer's valuable time to get the form completed. But it allowed us to be more precise in our pricing, taking out cross-subsidies in the rating engines of our competitors, for the benefit of us and our customers.

In short, it all came down to looking at the world in a different way from how everyone else was looking at it and not being afraid to try new things.

There are a thousand stories about those early years. There was internal conflict and conflict with the parent company. The parent company figured out that the 20 percent they'd given management could actually be quite valuable and they worked to get it back. At one point we surreptitiously got a major US insurer to make a bid for us, which the parent company refused. In the end, the legal process worked in our favor and after a few very difficult years we had clear title to the value we were creating. I'll stop there with all the dramatics of those early years. Join me for lunch or a beer and I'll tell you more.

For this current chapter, let's start the recap with this:

Three great myths of startups

1. You must be first. Guess what: There were a dozen search engines before Google.

And Admiral was the seventh UK company to go into direct-response car insurance. Frankly, I prefer it when other companies pave the roads for us to drive down.

2. You must be better at everything than your competition. That might help, but it wasn't the case for us. We were pretty poor at many things—we even forgot to create a customer services department until we started getting after-sales letters from customers! No, Admiral's early success was down to our choice of target market.

3. You make your own luck. Rubbish. That can happen, but luck is… well, luck. We had some excellent startups in other countries that didn't hold a candle to the UK success. Not because their businesses were poorly run, but because their market was in a very different place when they launched. In the UK we got lucky.

THE START OF SOMETHING BIG

The rough beginning of Admiral included a bitter lawsuit by "Disaffected Shareholders," leading to many tense days at the office and many nights of angst and misery. Often I asked myself if I should just pack up and move on. Why didn't I quit?

I stayed because of loyalty to all the people who were working so hard to make Admiral great. I knew that I could walk away and I'd be fine, but what might happen to them? I stayed because we were creating a good business. Hell, we were creating a great business. And I knew that if I could look past the war with certain managers and the other war with the parent company, Admiral was actually a lot of fun. We were doing things differently in an age when the term "disruptor" didn't exist. So I stayed.

Sure enough, once the Disaffected Shareholders left Admiral the remaining people pulled together and became a fantastic team. Everyone worked for the success of the venture, putting their individual interests second. Everyone had a role to play in the success of Admiral and everyone knew that his or her role was important to the success of the whole. The School of Hard Knocks provided far more challenges than I could have possibly imagined, but I learned a lot and kept moving forward.

Glad I stayed!

One story to tell. When we hired the underwriter he said he could also bring his claims manager, Dave W. (yes, yet another David!), with him. We interviewed a number of people for the job but the underwriter was bringing a lot of pressure for his guy. Dave W. was from the North of England and he had a very strong northern accent. He must have thought I was deaf because every third word he said found me saying, "What?" "Hunh?" Despite not being able to understand most of his sentences, we hired him.

When the underwriter left the organization I wondered if Dave W. would be leaving with him. I called him in and asked, and he told me no; he said he liked it here and he asked if he could stay, if that was OK.

That was a wonderful moment for me. He chose the organization we were building over following someone he'd worked with for many years. He was a fantastic claims manager with an amazing work ethic, which all went on to help us create that huge competitive advantage.

Dave W. is the kind of person anyone would want to help build a strong company from the inside out. In Part 2 of this book, I hope to show you how you can be that kind of manager—and how you can find and hire more like him.

Checklist for lift-off

Ask for the moon; you might get it. ☐

But be ready to compromise. ☐

Succeed before expanding. ☐

Don't rush recruitment. ☐

Look at the world differently; zig when others zag. ☐

Find your target market and learn everything about it. ☐

But explore other segments to find opportunities. ☐

Ride out rough patches. ☐

Stay loyal to your people and your mission. ☐

Fasten your seatbelt. ☐

PART 2
PHILOSOPHY

THE FOUR PILLARS OF ADMIRAL CULTURE

Often I'll hear people talk about "the culture at Admiral" or "this is the way an Admiral manager is supposed to act" or "this is our culture." What does that really mean? Is there a simple definition of the Admiral culture? Yes, there is, but that won't stop me going on for the next 40 pages about the details that definition entails.

First and foremost is this: If people like what they do, they'll do it better.

Ask yourself a simple question: If all my staff were better at what they do than they are now, would the company be better off? Would my job be easier? So my goal from 1993 onwards—and your goal going forward—is this: If you're going to get people to do better, you have to go out of your way to make your company / department / team a place they like.

It's common sense, really. Think about the things you've done really well in your life. I'll bet that most of them were things you liked doing. It's only in the odd circumstance that you did something really well that you didn't like. Positive energy is more likely to create positive results.

I say this confidently because I have the receipts. Admiral has gone from scratch to £3 billion of turnover. In our first 26 years we made profits of more than £3 billion. On average, that's over £300,000 every single day for 26 years!

Admiral now trades in five countries. Admiral created leading price comparison businesses. From that standing start in 1991, Admiral now has a value circa £9 billion and has paid more than £3 billion in dividends along the way.

That first year, 1993, we broke through all our budgets and re-forecasts and had income of £17 million. We got to the end of the year and thought we were kings of the world. Admiral now generates that every 44 hours.

So it's obvious that people at Admiral are doing their jobs very well. And why are they doing their jobs so well? (You can flip back a few paragraphs if you've forgotten.) That's right—they like what they do.

The proof in this case is not just in the numbers. For 20-plus years, the *Sunday Times* has compiled its list of the Best Companies to Work For. There is only one company that's made the list all 20-plus years. You get one guess. We win similar accolades in Italy, Spain, France, India, and the US. (There's a complete list in the Appendix.) A couple of years ago Admiral was named one of the 25 Best Companies in the World to Work For. In the world.

Personally, I was named the *Sunday Times* Best Big Company Leader three times running, from 2014 to 2016, and David won the following three years. (I'd better get this manual out there before he does his!)

I take great pride in being part of the success story that is Admiral Group. So many people have contributed to making Admiral successful. One key aspect is building the culture that helps propel our success.

I was the CEO from my joining the managing agent at Lloyd's in June 1991 until my semi-retirement in May 2016. I was part of the team (… the Team, the Team) that created a successful business. There are a large number of people who made Admiral what it is today. I'm just one of them. But society tends to think in terms of individuals. I believe CEOs get far too much credit when things go well, while also getting far too much blame when things go badly.

Success and failure of companies is down to the efforts of many people. It's the staff—you—who make it happen (or not!). Why does Admiral reward staff with shares? I'll go into this in more detail later but just suffice it to say we want staff to feel like they're owners. The best way to achieve that? Give them a piece of the company to own!

It's truly the right thing to do considering how much time and what a big part of your life work is. Plus, it's great motivation to know that when you do something well you are helping increase the value of your company; helping not only yourself, but everyone around you as well. Money might not buy happiness, but I can tell you that a rising share price does wonders for the mood in the office! Awards are great, but they just show that David and I were correct about building a happy culture. Making Admiral a place where people like to work helps those people do their best, which in turn rewards customers, employees, and investors. Talk about a virtuous circle!

PHILOSOPHY

Did I start my career all those years ago in Chicago with this philosophy? No. I didn't have a clue. My management philosophy has been sculpted over time. I mentioned before that you can read this book until the cows come home but that won't make you a great manager. You need to have experiences that will shape your style and beliefs. Reading this book can help you be aware of things, can help push you to think more about your style and beliefs. It's a bit of a shortcut, that's all.

I wish I'd had such a shortcut about 30 years ago. It would have spared me a number of mistakes I made along the way.

A culture is a complex, living organism, constantly changing and evolving. And when it comes to interpreting and implementing a culture, there's a huge open space with lots of room for mistakes.

There's a lot more to the Admiral culture than trying to make everybody happy every day. The end result has to be focused on creating the best results possible. Is your culture doing that? If your results aren't what you want them to be, maybe you should take a hard look at your culture.

One pet peeve of mine: Don't mistake a softer, people-oriented culture for a "weak" culture. The Admiral culture is definitely about people: caring for people, helping people, rewarding people, challenging people. We may seem soft because we are so focused on helping people—helping them succeed, to help the business succeed. Admiral is known to give people second chances and sometimes third chances. When someone has a problem, managers start by thinking, "How can I help this person succeed?"

But trying to help people doesn't mean, at any time, that you should accept shoddy work or lack of effort. That's not helping anybody. By all means, the Admiral way is that managers go out of their way to improve the performance of those around them, but they do not sacrifice their standards for this.

THE FOUR PILLARS OF ADMIRAL CULTURE

Part of the Admiral culture is great results—and you don't get great results from poor work. If people can't improve then they need to do something that's a better fit for their abilities or leave the company. That's part of my philosophy, too—which you'll learn about in this section of the book.

Yes, Admiral looks like a warm, cuddly place to work. But actually everything is measured and those that don't perform, despite repeated attempts to help them, don't stick around.

One thing we've learned is that culture is scalable. Turns out that "big" doesn't have to mean "unfeeling." When we were a relatively small company and had a great culture, some people said, "Just wait until you're bigger, then your culture goes." Rubbish! When we got to 750 people, we still had a great culture. Then over a thousand and we still had a great culture. And even today, with some 10,000 people, Admiral has a great culture.

Now it's true that creating and maintaining a great culture is harder as you get bigger—much harder, because you have to get buy-in and consistency from more and more people. I hope to show you how to accomplish that in the chapters that follow. But please, do not tell me that it's not possible. Don't say it and don't believe it. You just have to work harder to make it happen, that's all.

And yet, sometime in the 2000s, I felt Admiral had grown so big that I couldn't be sure that everyone knew just what our culture was, what it meant, and how managers should act in line with it. I felt the need to encapsulate this idea of "the Admiral Culture."

I came up with the following: The Four Pillars of Admiral Culture. Pillars sounds grandiose—you think of temples, cathedrals, monuments—but I want you to think of them as something managers can lean on. They support your company— and you.

There is a lot more depth in every culture than four pillars —that's the bit that sits on the pillars! But every business needs its pillars to unite its managers. Above the pillars there can be a lot of differences between departments, offices, etc. But everything throughout the organization, be it a startup of 10 people or a global giant of 200,000, can rest on those pillars. What follows are the four pillars of Admiral's culture.

Got it? OK, get ready to dive in. (Don't skip to the fun part just yet.)

THE FOUR PILLARS
OF
ADMIRAL CULTURE

1

COMMUNICATION

2

EQUALITY

3

REWARD

4

FUN

Before we start, however, I want to use this pillar metaphor to emphasize something important: Pillars hold up other structures. The pillars remain the same across the Admiral Group—but the rest of the structure is going to vary from place to place, department to department.

Admiral now reaches across much of the globe from its headquarters in Cardiff, Wales. But Admiral doesn't want to force everyone to conform to the same culture. That won't work. There are many differences between Cardiff and Swansea, let alone Cardiff and Delhi! What works in Cardiff won't necessarily work in Seville. We believe in local cultures all resting on those four pillars.

Embracing a local culture, the specific traits of a country or city, allows Admiral to operate more efficiently and with more energy. I believe in nurturing small groups rather than trying to create one large, cohesive group. Big groups can make employees feel like needles in the haystack, with little chance of being noticed or feeling effective. Forcing every office to adhere to one set of rules can create that feeling.

Many years ago I walked into the call center of a competitor, a huge open space with hundreds of people wearing headsets. I came away feeling that no one could possibly feel important in such an office. Worse, it must've been very easy to hide there—you could do nothing all day and I doubt anyone would notice. Hidden in plain sight!

That's why I have always been keen to keep things as small as possible. This requires a level of trust, because when you keep things small, you are giving the leader of a smaller group a lot of influence.

A company is a reflection of its management. I believe this because I see this all the time. And within a company, when you drill down into the many teams, you see the influence of all the layers of management, from the most distant to that with the most direct contact with those being managed.

This will sound obvious, but it hit me in a eureka moment: What managers and leaders do actually makes a difference in results! A great manager will get better results. In a bit I'll explain the three things you need to be a great manager.

Too often we get lost in a maze of spreadsheets and data and lose sight of the one thing that matters most of all: the motivation and care of the people who make the numbers happen. Those numbers on the spreadsheet don't happen because someone presses a button on a keyboard. They happen because people do things to make them happen. Only then does someone drop the number into the spreadsheet.

People naturally form groups. My positive concept of tribalism works on at least three levels: from department to department, from place to place, and from person to person. Admiral must accept that its Claims department will have a different culture than its Sales department. And, given different leaders, the Claims department in Swansea will be different from the Claims department in Cardiff, which will, in turn, be different from the Customer Services (CS) department in Cardiff. Obviously, different personality types are attracted to different jobs in different departments. CS people are different from claims people, claims people are different from salespeople, and salespeople are different from—well, you might say salespeople are different from everybody. Seriously, salespeople are different from IT people, and so on.

Furthermore, people are different by geography. People in each country are raised in a certain way, educated in a certain style, and that makes them different from people in the country next door. In the US the differences are from area to area, even state to state. The idea that you can just force people from around the world to be the same is crazy. Accept that there will be different behaviors across borders. Accept that a joke in one place might make people angry in another.

There's more: Every leader is different. Now I'm looking at you. That's why the Claims department in Swansea is different from Claims in Cardiff, which is different from Claims in Newport. If you dig even further, you'll find differences between each team—even in the same location—because each team manager is different from his or her peer.

About now you might be looking for the company's mission statement—a grand unifying proclamation that every manager in every location can turn to as a reminder of what we stand for. Well, you can stop looking.

We tried for 10 years to come up with one. It seemed the noble thing to do. After all, we were on a mission, right? After a decade of trying and failing to encapsulate the culture in a statement, we decided that we would try no more. Sorry, no mission statement. It gave us more time to do the important stuff.

We had lofty goals and ambitions, of course, so why not commit them to paper for all to see? We naturally wanted to show how dedicated we were to customers, staff, shareholders, and other stakeholders. But when we'd start the actual writing, it would turn into goody two-shoes language: We love our customers, we love our staff, we love our love, blah, blah, blah. Or the sentences would become potentially contradictory and hypocrisy-inducing: We will be brilliant for our customers, we will have a successful business, we will be good members of the community, etc.

But if we wrote "We will always give great service to every customer" (sounds nice, right?), what happens on the occasion that we don't? Our staff look at the mission statement and they think the company is run by a bunch of hypocrites.

For example, let's say we target 92 percent of our calls to be answered within 60 seconds. That's a good balance between serving customers and not being over-staffed. But that target means that 8 percent of our customers do not get great service. But it's inefficient to answer 100 percent of the calls. Aha! You are now caught between the proverbial rock and a hard place: You can't live up to your mission statement if you do what's right for the business. Or you have to do something that isn't good for the business but meets the terms of the mission statement. (In the end, what isn't good for the business isn't good for customers.)

So we decided we would just live our values. We believed that we must have a good financial performance, because that would save customers hassle and money now and in the future. And we believed that we would get that good financial performance if we looked after our customers. Further, we believed that to look after our customers to a pretty high standard, we needed to look after our staff to a very high standard. Those were our values and our modus operandi.

Much better, we concluded, to believe in these things and live them day-to-day rather than write something that tries to please everybody and probably is ignored by most.

This all goes back to culture. Admiral installed its four pillars everywhere in the Group, but we left space above them. This allowed every manager to add his or her own personality to the mix. The result is that when you walk into an Admiral office anywhere in the world, you pretty much know you're in an Admiral office, yet no two offices are the same.

OK, the pillars are up, the structure is built, and the place is humming. Let's step inside Admiral culture.

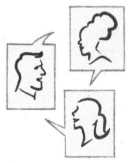

CHAPTER 6

GOOD MORNING!

When I look back on all the problems I've had—with customers, staff, peers, suppliers, even family and friends—those problems almost always come back to bad communication at some point in the chain.

Communication, communication, communication. You can almost never over-communicate.

Communication does not have to be complex. Start first thing in the morning—just say "Good morning" to everyone you meet. Then "Goodnight" to everyone you see as you leave in the evening. Just these two simplest of messages will start to make you a good communicator.

When I say "everyone you meet" I mean *everyone*! Whether it's the person who cleans the loo or your boss. They are all playing a part in the success of your team—and the company. Don't want to bother with someone who just cleans the loo? Try giving them a week off and then see how important they are to your organization!

This behavior pays dividends. If you ignore someone every morning on your way to your desk, they will probably ignore you back. But if you take a couple of seconds to say "Good morning" then they might open up and tell you something important. That simple "Good morning" shows that you're approachable, that communication is possible—and that can mean a great deal to the flow of information.

This pillar of Admiral's culture, communication, is transparent, invisible. Admiral has no managerial offices. Mine was the last one to go. You can go to our offices in Delhi, Halifax, Seville—wherever—and you will not find any manager offices.

Open plan is a great way to communicate. What do offices do? What do walls do? They are there for a purpose: to keep people out, to keep sound out, to separate people. What value is this separation? If you need to have a private word, use a meeting room. Why would you want to be separated from your colleagues? Why wouldn't you want to be seen?

This always puzzles me. Every business faces the challenges of competitors, changes in economic conditions, governments, perplexing consumer behavior, regulators, and so on. And yet many companies create unnecessary tension in their offices. Aren't all those outside forces enough to deal with?

Now I can see some fields that require privacy and deep, focused concentration, but even then, offices are barriers to communication. If privacy is key, then have more private cubicles, but don't completely shut off access. More on this in Chapter 7 on equality.

Good communication gets more people solving problems. Remember, the power of a team is greater than the power of any single individual (c'mon, that was only a few chapters ago!). The more people you have thinking about how to solve problems, the more likely you are to come up with better solutions.

My advice? Sit where you can see other people, where you can call out to them, and they can see and call you. But there's a lot more to communication than just being available. I like to encourage more communication with tea parties or friendly forums. Here you just get a group of people together, often from various areas of the company (they can be people who report directly to you or not) and chat for 90 minutes over a cup of tea. These are wide-open meetings, no agenda. I always came with a few questions to ask, but usually a discussion started and no prodding was needed. They can ask you anything and you can ask them anything.

For larger numbers, I found online chats valuable. Here I would log in and so would hundreds of staff. The staff could ask me anything they wanted. Sometimes the questions were very challenging—Why did we do this or that?—while others were lighter, about baseball (Go Cubs!) or my favorite singers. (I used to be a deadline sportswriter, and can still type at 50 words per minute, so even when the questions piled up I was able to get to them all!)

When I took over as the CEO of our US insurance operation in 2017, I created a "Tell Henry" email address. This was private—anyone could ask me anything, without having to do it in front of hundreds of staff on a chat line, and I would get back to them straight away. At first this was used a lot but as time went on people found it easier to speak up publicly. A very positive change stimulated by opening the channel of communication.

Then there are the mass communications, like a company

or department intranet for the lighter side of work, which also highlights births, weddings, pets, whatever. For the last 20 years or so Admiral has done a Staff General Meeting (SGM). This is where we get everyone in the company together in a single day (could be several shows to ensure business continuity) and give them all the same message.

The SGM is a combination of business information—targets, goals, review of past performance—and lighthearted entertainment from managers. David always endeared himself by doing a segment vaguely related to the business that would usually involve relationship advice or the like. He always took on an identity for the bit, one requiring a costume—a handyman, say, or Superman—and they were always hilarious (just don't mention lederhosen to him).

Some people dread meetings. Not me.

Meetings are another good way to communicate. I retired as Group CEO in May 2016. In March 2017 I served as the temporary CEO of Elephant, our US insurance business. I found the organization extremely... organized. So much so that everyone was deep in their own silo. No one seemed to talk with anyone!

The previous August I'd spent a month in the US, primarily with Elephant. I saw then that the organization needed more communication. I convinced the then-CEO to have morning meetings, every morning, with his senior team.

Virtually the entire Elephant organization was on just two floors of one building. This should be a huge advantage in communication. Think of all the competitors who have managers in several buildings scattered across one city—or possibly all over the country, in different time zones, maybe even in different countries. Elephant had everyone in one place. So when I visited again a few months later, I was eager to sit in on a couple of those morning meetings.

They were dreadful. They depressed me, and I wasn't even part of the team. I can't imagine how they affected those managers who bothered to show up. The few who did would spend a few minutes with joyless chat, perhaps about yesterday's results, but nothing of substance. The meetings lasted less than 15 minutes but felt far longer! They were clearly just going through the motions so they could say they had a meeting every morning.

How could we fix this? I returned in March with a few ideas, keen to make these meetings valuable.

Step 1: Tell them they don't have to come.

Wait, what? That's right, the meeting was never compulsory. I had all the senior managers who were around on a given day get together at 8.45 am. At first, only six were invited, but then a couple of people who were in the next layer of management asked if they could join. Sure. Why not? Some managers asked if they could bring other managers from their departments. Sure. Why not? And we would discuss the issues of the business. Certainly we would look at results, but we also took the time to discuss how we were trying to change the results.

Step 2: Use an imaginary table.

You can find one anywhere, cheap. We sat in a circle in a large, open meeting area. After a few weeks of this we had 20 or 30 people attending. Not only would we talk about current issues, but we'd also have deeper discussions like, "How are decisions made in this company?" (A great question that yields surprising answers.) We were getting input from different departments, different levels of management. Key word: different.

Step 3: Turn off the clock.

We got rid of minutes, in more ways than one. There was no time limit, so some mornings the meetings went on for more than an hour. And some lasted but 10 minutes. The point is that timed meetings sometimes are forced to go longer than needed and people can come away thinking they were time-wasters. Or they're cut short and important issues don't get discussed fully enough. After a while we started to type up a record of what got discussed, which went to all managers. So if you weren't there, you still knew what was going on. A few months later we started sending the notes to everyone in the company. Why not? And that still happens. Every morning.

How to cook up solutions

Don't have time for open-ended meetings? Bring an egg timer. I like my meetings like my eggs: three minutes. You'll be surprised how much valuable information can be conveyed in 180 seconds. (Of course, you can extend it if necessary.)

You can discuss a new movie, last night's football match, or talk about an IT release that went live the day before. It's a great chance for a manager to put their stamp on the team, to motivate and inspire the staff. Everyone leaves the meeting wanting today to be better than yesterday.

Try it—even a short meeting can yield better performance. And I'm sure you can now find an egg timer app.

One manager told me that he'd ask one randomly chosen person a good question each day. His best question was, "What did you do yesterday to make a difference for a customer?" I love that question! It prods someone to think about the good things they've done, and it gives the group a positive story before they all dig in for the day. And I love that everyone else is thinking, "Gosh, I'd better do something good today in case it's my turn tomorrow!"

This is crucial: Use the end of the meeting to make sure people are inspired. You've had your discussions. You've talked about the results and what's needed. You've heard a good story on how a customer was helped. Now it's your moment. The egg is almost cooked. Your team are getting ready to do their job for the day. How would you like them to go back to their desks? Happy and inspired? Ready to do great things?

This is a motivation moment. A chance to give your people that little boost that means they'll do just a bit better all day long. Maybe it's challenging them to do better than they did yesterday. Maybe challenge them to smile non-stop for the next 60 minutes. (It's hard! But people are naturally friendlier when they are smiling.) If you can motivate and inspire your people at the beginning of the day, they are likely to perform better *all* day. The end of the meeting is your moment. Don't waste it.

These meetings went a long way toward helping an organization that was dysfunctional in its communication become one of the best communicating groups I've ever seen.

It was gratifying to see unexpected benefits arise from these meetings. As people communicated more, they became more tolerant of each other and tolerant of mistakes and problems. In their previous world if someone had a problem, that was their problem. And everyone else looked away. Better him than me! Now when someone raised a problem, the first thing people in the circle said was, "How can I help?" Or they'd relate how they dealt with a similar problem.

You can't imagine the difference this made. They knew they weren't going to get bashed or ignored if they had a problem. In fact, they were going to get others to help them sort out the problem. And they communicated even more. It was a virtuous circle. Around that imaginary table, you had more minds thinking about a problem—and you know how much better a team is than an individual, right? Smart solutions abounded.

The Welcome Talk

From the very beginning of Admiral I made a point to meet with every new starter who came into the UK business. At first, it was on their first morning. But I got pretty busy and they were getting overloaded with information, so we put my talk back to sometime in their first week, then their first month.

Eventually I was doing so many "Welcome Talks" that I'd wait until we had 40 or more starters to meet (even then there were times when I'd do this talk five times in a month!). I've probably done my Welcome Talk more than 600 times in front of 20,000 people spanning 25 years.

And I loved it. I loved it because I made sure that every member of staff understood how important they were to our success. I loved it because it gave me the opportunity to tell people what Admiral stood for. I loved it when each person took a minute to introduce him or herself.

One thing I found fascinating was their answer to my question: Why did you leave where you were to join Admiral?

I was shocked by much of what I heard about former employers. Many people said they left because they weren't treated right. I'd ask for more, and this is what I heard:

"Treated like dirt."

"Managers didn't work but pushed everyone else really hard."

"Had to ask permission to go to the toilet (which was sometimes refused)."

"No respect."

"No appreciation."

"Nobody cared."

I'm sure that if I asked the CEOs of these companies, some of them well-known, national organizations, why they treated their people badly they'd give a big "Harrumph! People are our most important asset!"

My Welcome Talk themes

- The customer, the customer, the customer. We're all here for the customer because the customer pays all the bills.
- The inverted pyramid of importance. If the customer is the most important person in the company, who's next? Hint: The CEO and the board are at the bottom of the inverted pyramid. I tell them loud and clear: I am here to support you, not the other way around. Your managers and team leaders are here to support you. Not the other way around.
- The power of each individual. I challenge each of them to do something with their talent.
- The power of talented individuals working together. The Team, the Team, the Team. I give them all a piece of a jigsaw puzzle (we went through a lot of puzzles in 25 years!), telling them that no individual makes the puzzle. We put all the pieces together; that's how we see the big picture. We are all in this together.

Clearly those CEOs are way too far from their actual work-force, and their message isn't really cascading down, now, is it?

Lesson learned? Get close to your people. They are talking to your customers, they are making sales, they are programming your system. What could be more important? Who is paying the bills? The customer. Logically, then, who could be more important than the people communicating with customers, either directly, via email, marketing messages, or computer code? So make them feel important. Because they are!

The more senior you are in the organization, the more times you should meet with people. Don't have the time? Make the time. People feel important when senior managers pay attention to what they do. So pay attention!

I made note cards for that first talk in 1992, rewrote them in 1999 and never revised them again.

One time I arrived for a Welcome Talk in Swansea and realized I had left my note cards in Cardiff. I had done this talk hundreds of times so surely I rattled it off from memory, right? Wrong. It was a total mess! I left things out, mixed up the order of other comments. Never forgot my note cards again!

We're always trying to forecast the future of our business, which is tricky at best. But you can control one aspect of that forecast by welcoming in new staff to your team or your company. They are your future. Explain to them what you're all about and what the organization is all about; what they should expect from you and the organization. Ask them—and then listen carefully—why they chose to work for you.

The feedback loop

Everyone craves feedback. We all want to know: How are we doing? We almost don't care if the feedback is positive or negative (although we prefer positive); we just want to know where we stand.

I'm a big believer in appraisals—upwards, downwards, and sideways. When I was doing appraisals for the people I managed directly, I would seek out feedback from people on their level, people they managed, people they worked with, *et al.*, to add to my own observations and thoughts.

And yes, I got appraisals, too, which I always looked forward to. Two brave people who reported to me would gather feedback, both quantitative and qualitative, from the entire team, whether they reported directly to me or not, and tell me what I could do better. Sometimes they told me things that I would have preferred not to hear. But I knew that the only way I could improve was to

Appraising behavior

Treat an appraisal like the special event that it is for the person you are appraising. You might appraise 15 different people but this one is their only one.

- Schedule it well in advance and block off plenty of time.
- Don't cancel unless you're, say, giving birth. Canceling is a great demotivator.
- Turn your phone off and never look at your watch.

Remember: This is a big moment for the employee, unlike regular meetings. This is when you really focus on the person. If the discussion splinters off, which it will, bring it back to the person.

listen to their feedback, think about what it meant, and do whatever needed to be done. Funny, it was always two different people each year!

Here's the feedback I remember best: I was inconsistent in my decision-making. I'm like anyone, I can gripe about criticism. In this case, well, the opposite of that critique would be that I was a stubborn decision-maker. Second, they couldn't give me specifics because that would blow the cover of anonymity crucial to feedback.

So I couldn't know if my perceived inconsistency was the result of, say, receiving new information—or because the wind was out of the north-east that day. Didn't matter, in the end. Even if I didn't see the complaint myself, it was actually a complaint about my communication. If I was changing a decision because of new information, then I needed to communicate that, not just change the decision.

Feedback brings you down to earth. We all want to feel like we're doing a brilliant job. But that's not always the way it's perceived by those we work with. You've got to suppress your ego for a bit, listen, and then make a plan of what you'll do differently—so that next appraisal you'll get improved feedback.

Don't fret over giving bad news. Many times I would have a manager in a regular one-to-one meeting say he was dreading Bob's appraisal next Tuesday because he had some tough messages to pass to Bob and maybe Bob would be upset, or even quit. We'd spend 20 minutes on how to deliver the tough news and mulling how Bob would react.

And then I'd see this manager the following week and ask, "How did it go?" "What?" "Bob's appraisal." "Oh, fine." "What about the tough messages?" "Oh, he was fine." That was it. All that angst for nothing! We all want to know how we are doing, even if that includes bad news.

Before I did anyone's appraisal, I always held one thing in my mind. Do you know what that might be? No, it wasn't their performance: I knew that going in (and so did they!). No, it wasn't whether I had all the feedback; I did.

Let me flip all the cards over. The main thing on my mind was: How could I get the employee to leave the appraisal more energized than when they came in? Regardless of whether I had good messages, tough messages, or a combination of messages to deliver, I wanted every person I appraised to walk out of that appraisal keen to do a better job than when they walked in.

I also keep in mind four magic words to achieve the above goal, especially when there were tough messages involved: You... can... do... better.

These are powerful words. Here's why:

YOU makes it clear who this is directed at. And, face it, we all like hearing and talking about ourselves.

CAN is a sign of belief. I believe you can; it's not a hope or a wish, it's a belief. It's also positive. I'm not saying "might" or "have the potential," I'm saying "You can."

DO is an active verb. This isn't something you think about, or plan, or discuss—it's something you "do."

BETTER doesn't mean you're doing badly (although that's possible!) but says that there is more in the tank, more you can get from your talent.

Taken together, when you lock onto someone's eyes and say, quite slowly and deliberately, "You... can... do... better," it's very likely that they will leave the meeting keen to prove you right, believing that they actually can, and will, do better.

Doing better is not to be mistaken for trying harder. Trying harder might help someone to do better, but there are people who try hard all the time who also need to do better. What you want from everyone, even those who give a great effort, is a better performance.

You should never shy away from giving a tough message, but

you want the person to leave in a positive frame of mind. This is a skill that takes time and practice.

And if it's a star performer and you don't have much criticism, these words can still work. Just preface them with: How do you think you can do better? And star performers are likely to know where they can improve better than you!

The receiving end

What about feedback for you? Make sure your manager appraises you. You also need to know how other people see you—those who work for you, those who you work alongside. Ideally your manager has gathered that input.

But on your own you can try this trick: Ask people to describe your brand.

Believe it or not, you are building a brand as a manager. A manager's brand is the promise he or she makes to his reports—so they know what to expect when they work with you. Before you do this, write down what you think others will say your brand is.

Then send all these people a request for feedback. Start by asking them what they think the McDonald's brand is. This gets them thinking about the difference between a brand and merely a list of strengths and weaknesses. They might say that the McDonald's brand stands for food fast and cheap, kid-friendly, clean bathrooms, etc. How about Tiffany's brand? Expensive, glamorous, and so on. It doesn't matter what they say, it's just to get them thinking about brands. Then ask them what your brand is.

Recruit someone neutral to gather replies to ensure anonymity. Don't just look at the brand values they list; but also look for common threads. Do they see you in the same light? If they do come up with similar values—hey, good or bad, at least you're consistent! Or do you get a wide range of replies, meaning you are different things to different people? There's no right or wrong. But it might help you to know how you are coming across to people. Then compare what people say about you with what you thought they'd say. How does that look?

As a manager, it's tempting and easy to avoid being critiqued. Getting honest feedback is a challenge. You have to work at it. Be creative in the ways you search for it. But keep searching. Don't stop. It's difficult to improve if you don't know what people think of your current behavior.

Going big

Surveys are a form of communication. Admiral enters all the Best Company to Work For contests it can find. Admiral is keen to be measured against other companies and, let's face it, it's nice to be known as a great company to work for.

But the main reason Admiral enters these things is that we get a huge amount of quantitative data on what our staff like and don't like, what management does well and what it, well, can do better(!).

Some companies resist such contests because they're afraid of what they might learn. Or they worry about not making the list or placing below their competition. But in this instance ignorance is definitely not bliss. If you want to improve your company's performance, you need to know what's really going on.

For many years, before these contests even came about, we did our own Annual Staff Survey. Start this early on because when you do something annually, the data points come slowly. You need to find your base level quickly so in future years you can gauge progress.

Some companies don't share this information with staff. I think that's crazy. It will be to your benefit to share as much information as possible with the greatest number of people. Of course, not everyone will benefit, but you'd be surprised how many people are genuinely interested in how their team, their department, their company, is doing. Yet so many companies hide information from staff as if they were competitors. If you want people to be involved you cannot treat them like mushrooms.

Feedback in the PA system

Everyone has flaws as a leader and manager. One of mine was that I didn't push back enough when I saw things that weren't right. I'd think maybe they were right and trust that they knew best. Too often, I should have trusted my own judgment and said something.

Once I sent our IT manager an email and got a response from his personal assistant (PA). Then I called him but just got his PA on the phone. Hmm. This wasn't exactly Admiral style.

You know how I feel about offices and walls. PAs can also be walls. I admit, I have had a PA since nearly the beginning. But I shared my PA with other managers and unless I was in a meeting I took my calls myself; she did not have access to my emails. She spent most of her time booking travel, organizing events, getting me to meetings on time, ushering visitors to the right place, preparing papers, etc. I was adamant that she would not be a filter between me and my team.

By the time of this incident I was busy with our non-UK businesses and David was focused on the UK business. I was surprised when it took days for the IT manager to get back to me.

This wasn't right. This wasn't how our managers should communicate, but I didn't do anything about it. My mistake. It took us a couple of years to figure out that this manager wasn't doing a great job. Part of that was his lack of communication with other parts of the organization. I had the evidence in my lap years before we reached that conclusion.

I should have kicked up a fuss, told him he couldn't build a PA wall to separate him from those who needed his attention. I should have told him that's not how an Admiral manager managed. I failed him and the organization. If the CEO doesn't get a response inside 48 hours what hope does the average manager or member of staff have? I knew it was wrong when it happened but I failed to act upon this knowledge.

Two lessons here: One, walls come in many forms but always inhibit communication; and two, sometimes you have to speak up when you see things that aren't right.

Once a CEO of one of our businesses called me to say, "We've had some bad results lately and lost a big supplier. Do you think I should tell my senior managers?" I said, "Of course you should tell them! Your people will know that things aren't right just from the way you look. Share the good times and share the bad times." Nothing could be worse than saying one thing while others know from your body language that you're covering something up.

Stupid things we do

Let me wrap up this section with a communications story that involves customers, staff, managers, IT, small meetings, huge meetings, lots of phone calls, and a special email address. You might want to cue up "Communication Breakdown" by Led Zeppelin while you read it.

Everyone listen to this

Here's a communication story that starts bad but ends happy. Early on, we once messed a customer about pretty badly, leaving them waiting at the DVLA for hours, among other nightmares. And all the conversations were on tape.

I listened to all the tapes myself, becoming incensed at the succession of errors. Nobody took ownership of the problems or worked to sort them out. It kept getting passed from pillar to post. I got every manager in the organization together (it took at least three shows) and played them the tapes. I didn't need to add much, except to say I was horrified by this service, it would not be tolerated, and if the people in the room weren't ready to do far better, then I'd find people who were.

It didn't matter if it wasn't their department; it could have easily been theirs. This was everyone's problem. Service levels improved.

One of the ancillary products Admiral was selling after making the car insurance sale was breakdown cover, also known as roadside assistance. We had several levels of breakdown cover to sell, e.g. basic cover and then cover that included home start. When we'd sell a basic breakdown cover, we'd wait a few days and then try to upgrade the customer to the next level of breakdown. Lots of customers opted for the higher level. But the system wasn't working correctly. It was not only charging them more for the higher-level product, as it should, but it was also charging them £5 for canceling the standard product, the normal cancelation fee if they had canceled the policy of their own volition.

Wait a minute. We call you to upgrade, then charge you for canceling the original product?! Oof. This can't be right.

We found out that some of our staff knew this was happening, and knew it was wrong (let's hope so!) because in about half the cases the £5 charge had been manually waived. But in the other half it sailed through.

What was the real problem? Yes, the system was flawed, but these things happen. The real problem was that this ridiculous practice had been going on for many months—some 30,000 cases! We had to send checks for £5 to 30,000 customers! Incredible. Drove me up the wall. Why weren't our staff screaming from the rafters about this?

Either nobody spoke up so nothing got done, or somebody spoke up but the team managers didn't do anything about it, or the team managers did something but nobody else took any notice or it was buried in some IT queue. But the blame game was beside the point.

The real problem was: communication, communication, communication. In this instance, we failed.

At the next Staff General Meeting I announced a special email address called Stupid Things We Do and told every member of the company to send me anything they thought was odd, stupid, or shameful.

I received some 500 emails. Fortunately, many of them over-lapped—there weren't 500 uniquely stupid things! Only one email was flippant. The rest were serious and well thought out.

I responded to every one of them myself, forwarding most of them to the manager of the department best placed to respond. I then made sure the manager reviewed the email and gave the person who sent it a prompt reply. Most of the emails were asking why we were doing certain things that they found difficult to explain to a customer. There were a few things where a simple change (usually some additional communication) could eliminate the problem.

More important than the fixes was conveying to staff the idea that if they saw something that looked a bit weird, they should scream. If it looks stupid, if it smells stupid, and you think it's stupid, it's probably stupid! And I hope it was clear that someone would listen. Me!

Here's a reminder. Communication, communication, communication. It's almost impossible to over-communicate. Am I repeating myself? Good.

Communication lines

✓ Greetings and goodbyes are important.
✓ Open office plans are best.
✓ Meet regularly, meet smart.
✓ Be creative in finding ways to communicate.
✓ Buy an egg timer. Have a tea party.
✓ Keep communication lines open.
✓ Respect your staff.
✓ Welcome newcomers. They are your future.
✓ Treat appraisals seriously. Everyone craves feedback.
✓ Remind everyone: You can do better.
✓ Remind yourself, too.
✓ Take surveys—and share the results.
✓ Don't hide bad news.

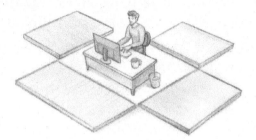

CHAPTER 7

TEARING DOWN THE WALLS

Once we were looking at buying a US company. Talks were proceeding nicely; the spreadsheets were working and there was a reasonable likelihood the deal would get done. Then we made a visit to their HQ in a major US city.

We walked into a modern glassy building and immediately saw that all the windows were blocked by offices, the entire way around the perimeter. Every manager had a window office, with a pleasant view of the blue sky and the city, and every single window was part of an office.

The middle of the floor was divided up with six-foot-tall partitions. So the non-managers came into an office with no natural light, and entered a space surrounded by six-foot-tall barriers to do their work. They must have felt like they were walking into vertical coffins!

That killed the deal. We saw that if we bought that company we'd have to tear down all of those offices, redesign the entire space into an open plan, and in so doing we'd probably lose most of the managers who were spoiled by their window offices and the status that went with them.

We let the deal drop. The managers would have struggled with the egalitarian culture that we strive for in Admiral.

I've already discussed how an open plan facilitates communication. In the same way, getting rid of offices is a tangible way to show how equality works in the organization.

Equality means different things in different contexts: political, social, racial, gender, economic, and so on. What does equality mean in a business context? For Admiral, it means trying to get rid of the often obvious divides between people. But I'm not being soft-headed about this. I may have come of age in the 1970s, but let's face it, businesses are not communes.

There are differences between people in the company, in particular what they are paid. Of course some people get paid more than others; some people also have more responsibility than others. But equality tries to ensure that we don't rub people's noses in these things. Why? Because everyone is important. Otherwise, why would we hire them? Everyone in the company has a role to play in its success.

Equality is our way of making sure—as best we can—that everyone is rowing in the same direction. I ask again: Isn't competition tough enough without doing things that divide your own company? I've seen some companies where there was more intense internal competition—fratricide—than there was with the external world! What a mess.

Inequality can show up anywhere:

Chairs: One organization I was in before Admiral had two types of chairs. The managers all had chairs with arms. The rest of the staff didn't. One time one of the chairs with arms went missing. We found it two days later, hidden away, and the arms had been bent out of shape! Even furniture can exacerbate feelings of inequality!

Cars: There are no company cars in Admiral, unless a car is required to do the job. Company cars are divisive. It starts with those who have them and those who don't. But it doesn't stop there. Who has a 3 Series and who has a 5 Series? I was in an organization where managers had 3 Series BMWs but the CEO drove a 7 Series. And he took not one but two car park spaces just in front of the door. Talk about sending messages of who's important here!

Lunch: There is no executive dining room in Admiral. Again, I've worked in an office that had an executive dining room with a chef who worked 15 hours a week and was paid the equal of a full-time sales agent. This was seriously divisive for the junior staff who had to walk past the dining room while the boozy lunches were going on. But it was also felt by the senior managers who were invited perhaps once a month versus those who were invited three times a week. Few things are more divisive than who gets invited to have port with cheese.

At one Welcome Talk a new recruit told me a story that crystalizes how too many companies operate. He said he worked in a call center (at another company!) where the staff were not allowed any food or drink at their desks—not even a glass of water. "That sounds harsh," I thought, but maybe the IT department was worried about its keyboards and computers. Seemed wrong to make everyone suffer for the sake of a few keyboards, but, OK, I could understand it.

Then this guy delivered the kicker: Every morning at 10.30 they would wheel a sterling silver tea service into the manager's office, and she would have tea and biscuits at her desk! Now maybe this manager is thinking she's being uber-efficient by working at her desk during tea break, not even getting out of her chair, but she clearly has no idea what kind of hypocritical message she's sending her employees.

Great managers must always examine the rules and be absolutely certain they can abide by them. In fact, they need to be rules leaders. The minute you start to have one rule for "them" and another for "us" you start to divide your workforce. Why would you want to do that? (Hint: You don't.)

Equality is certainly about getting rid of painful divisions but it's also about the way you treat people. It's not about treating everyone brilliantly, it's about treating everyone in the same way: fairly. And it means making sure everyone treats everyone else fairly as well.

Take pension programs, another natural source for separation. A lot of companies have better pension arrangements for senior managers than for other staff. Admiral's program is the same for all (except David and me, who get no pension contributions whatsoever from the company).

Equality means the managers don't always get the best views in the building. When we built our company headquarters, Ty Admiral, a few years ago, we could tell that the views from the top floors were going to be quite good, but the lower floors were going to look out on car parks and other buildings.

So David and I took space in the middle of the building, on floor six of 12. That way we would be closest to all staff, and the managers wouldn't dominate the top floor.

When the building opened, David and I went up to the top floor to have a look around. Sure enough, the views really were great. We looked at each other and without a word both started laughing. We were thinking the same thing: These views are brilliant! Did we make the right call on this one? Lol!

Of course we did. The people who are doing the heavy lifting in our company deserve the best views.

When I was acting CEO at Elephant, we had a problem with an important member of staff. This was a guy who had been with us six or seven years and was head of an important section of the Claims department. Hard worker, very intelligent, but he also thought a lot of himself and tried very hard to be clever, in a cynical sort of way. More to the point, he was known for being, well, let's just call it less than diplomatic on occasion. One day he burst into a meeting just as it was getting under way, already very angry. It seems he had been double-booked between that meeting and teaching a training class. He was irate about this double booking and felt it was the fault of the person who had booked him into the training class—who he'd now come to confront.

He let rip at her in front of everyone, let her know how unhappy he was, blamed her, and stormed out.

This was not the first time he'd stepped over the line; he had been reprimanded for treating people badly in the past.

Even though he was talented and dedicated, filling a valuable role, we had to let him go. There was no place in that company for someone who showed such disrespect for a colleague. That he held a higher position and made more money than the person he had an issue with was irrelevant. As human beings, they are equal, and he should have treated her that way. In fact, that he had a higher position meant he had an even greater responsibility to treat people decently.

It's worth repeating: Every member of staff must treat every other member of staff with dignity and respect at all times. There are no compromises on this. Everyone in our organization is important and deserves the respect of his or her colleagues.

Equal measures

✓ Equality should be part of the architecture.
✓ Help everyone row in the same direction.
✓ Minor offences can exacerbate inequality.
✓ Examine the rules and abide by them.
✓ A nice view isn't essential.
✓ Respect isn't just a song by Aretha.

CHAPTER 8

THE POWER OF APPRECIATION

Reward comes in many flavors. Money is clearly an important reward. After all, if they didn't pay you, you wouldn't work here, would you? I wouldn't!

Money gets you and me (and a whole lot of other people) to show up every day. But that's not enough. You want to be a great manager and, I assume, you also want yours to be a great company. Money alone won't make that happen.

To be great you need to appeal to people's emotional side, not just their wallet or purse. Do this well and you'll get the most from people: the most effort, the most loyalty, the most enjoyment and the most success. Keep in mind, everyone needs motivating.

Did you ever have a boss or teacher say something specifically nice to you about something you did? I'll bet you went home that night and told your Mom, Dad, partner, the dog—someone, everyone—about it. This was important to you. That you wanted others to know should tell you how valuable a good word is. That's it: a good word. Words are powerful. When used appropriately, they can be a motivating, positive force.

Managers have to learn how to say nice things to people. They also need to speak honestly, which can get tricky. Sometimes that means looking for the good in something that was perhaps not entirely good.

Do you really have to "learn" how to say nice things? Frankly, yes. It sounds easy but it's more complicated than it seems. First off, you have to make sure you're not just giving some bullshit compliment. People aren't stupid—they can see through false compliments like a cow can smell the barn. Second, be mindful of the others around. If you tell your team in a loud voice how brilliantly Bob has done by answering 10 calls this afternoon, make sure Freya hasn't answered 11 calls and is sitting right there, fuming and wondering why Bob is the teacher's pet.

You have to be conscious of everything you do and the effect on everyone around you. It's one of the reasons management is difficult to do well.

Here are two good words you should use every day: thank you. This is really basic but really important. (It's so simple that I feel I'm writing the business book equivalent of *Love Story* when I write this. Half a century ago, *Love Story* was a bestselling novel written by a Harvard professor. It was such a simple read that the author was seen as a traitor to all Harvard stands for. But, sometimes, simple is best.)

THE POWER OF APPRECIATION

There it is: Just say "thanks."

Among the problems I found at Elephant in 2017 was a lack of appreciation for what many people in the organization were doing. Remember those 8.45 am meetings I started? On the Thursday morning that first week I brought a package of thank-you cards and handed one to each of the senior managers. Their assignment: Find someone in the organization worthy of receiving it, hand-write a card and leave it for that person by the end of Friday.

They did as asked and the next week we repeated the exercise.

By the third week we had printed a postcard with an elephant motif saying "Thank You" on the front and I passed these around the circle, which had now grown to some 15 people. Most of the people took one.

After that I would just bring a stack of these postcards to the Thursday-morning meeting and managers would come up at the end of the meeting to get a card or two or three. Of course these cards—with handwritten notes—were now also turning up on people's desks all over the company. Staff were really touched that a manager, maybe even one from a different part of the company, had taken the time to write a card of thanks to them. I even received a thank-you card once from someone thanking me for sending them a thank-you card!

Quick question: When do you have the most energy—at the beginning of the day or the end? For most people, it's the beginning. Let's say the average person starts the day with an energy level of 100 and by the end of their shift it's down to 70. What if you could get them to start the day at 120? Then maybe their low point would be 90. Or maybe because they started higher, they might only drop to 99. Would 20 percent more effort from everyone you manage improve your results?

That's why it's important to motivate people first thing in the morning.

Another question: What's your morning routine? Probably something like this: Say hello, turn on the computer, grab a cup of coffee or tea, and sit down to emails. Good. But not good enough. You didn't light a fire under anybody. Your routine doesn't motivate anyone. You were nice, you were polite, but you weren't inspirational. This is why those morning meetings, even if just three minutes long, are so important. This is your opportunity to give your team that extra boost. You can't hit your targets yourself, so giving your people extra energy, extra motivation, gives you the best chance to meet your goals.

Just as there is no recipe that can tell you how to be a great manager, there is no formula for what kind of words will inspire someone. Different things will inspire different people at different times. Sometimes you need emotion, sometimes it's humor, sometimes targets and challenges—and these things can all be with the same group of people.

The one thing you always need to be is sincere. If you're talking about challenges, don't challenge people to do things that are blatantly impossible. I don't care how much inspiration you give me, I will never play second base for the Cubs (I'm left-handed!). To challenge me with that is absurd.

Use a variety of ways to inspire. Some days it's something near and dear to your heart, some days it's a silly joke to get people to relax, some days it could be a poem, some days it could be asking people what they dream of accomplishing. Be creative. See what works (and, equally important, what doesn't) with each person.

Think back again to when you did something really well, at work or in school. Tell me, did you do that thing really well because you were under threat ("If you don't get an A on that paper, you'll be grounded for a month!") or because you wanted to do well? Most of us do our best work when we want to, not when we're under threat. Do you really think your people are going to be much different?

Yes, you can get results from negative, bullying, threatening management. But they don't last. People close down after that initial fear-induced surge. When you appeal to their positive side, however, you get sustainable energy.

Now I've heard managers say, "Why should I thank someone for doing a good job? That's what I pay them for." This is at once true and short-sighted. Yes, we do hire people and pay them a salary and for that we expect good work in return. But that doesn't mean good work should be taken for granted. Even if it's paid for.

Everyone appreciates recognition for what they do above and beyond their contractual payment. As a great manager, the idea is to get more from your people. I'd argue that you don't get "more" when you assume a monthly bank deposit is more powerful than a monthly bank deposit and a "thank you." And, on the other side, what does it cost you to say "Thanks"?

So we've discussed the value of encouraging words—a little praise, a thank you, a good morning and a goodnight. There are other non-monetary rewards that are very powerful. Three in particular.

1. Responsibility

One of the hardest things for any manager to do is relinquish responsibility. As a manager, you probably understand this: You got to be a manager because you're better than others at certain tasks, usually those having to do with the job in question. Others are less qualified and less able—if not, they might have the manager job. (But remember—by delegating to them, they will become more qualified and more able. Give them a chance!)

Delegation is a skill to be learned, especially for a new manager. You must accept that when you delegate, their approach may differ from yours. Tasks might not be as well executed. Results might be less impressive.

But consider this—if you get someone else to do them, then you can do other, more important things. Think of yourself as a professor. A professor would not expect their students to produce the quality of work he or she could produce. But the professor is there to help the students get better at that work so that maybe one day, they can produce work of the same or better quality.

Part of the reticence to delegate is ego. You think you're the best in the office at a task, and maybe you are—at that point in time, anyway. I have a friend, now retired, who was a first-class reporter and editor. He could do the work of his staff better than they could. So he often performed their tasks, fixing this, fixing that, and hoarding responsibility. At the end of his career he realized that by doing other people's work, he may have done a disservice to workflow, staff improvement, and office morale. And, oddly, he may have done himself a disservice by limiting his role to "Mister Fix-It."

Here's where you can put your ego to work: The more you delegate responsibility, the more you can accomplish by moving on to bigger and better things. It allows you to spread your influence and enlarge your skill base. And always keep in mind the benefit to everyone from giving someone else responsibility. Think of when you were a child put in charge of something—making cookies, raking leaves, handing out books in class. I'll bet it made you feel like a million pounds (or dollars or euros).

When we give someone responsibility, we are demonstrating trust, and trust is a great motivator. Voilà, there's your bottom line: motivation. Now that's great managing!

2. Autonomy

This is more difficult to make work. When you give responsibility, you don't necessarily wash your hands of what happens. When you give autonomy, you let people get on with things with little or no interference.

Some people crave autonomy. Some people do well with autonomy. Unfortunately, the two groups are not always the same! So be careful. If you give autonomy to someone who will then listen to no one and just do what they want, you won't always get the best result. Alternatively, some people do very well, gathering ideas and synthesizing thoughts, without your prodding, and reach good conclusions.

At the same time, some people crave autonomy (low maintenance) but others don't really want to be on their own (high maintenance). In both instances, the quality of work can be good or bad. A manager must know their people—which ones will realize that it's a compliment to leave them alone and which ones will struggle if they think you're avoiding them.

3. Challenge

The third item in this trilogy is challenge. If you're a manager reading this manual, I'm pretty sure you crave challenge. It's one of the reasons you became a manager. Curiously, challenge is also an important part of reward. A leader needs to challenge people as a way to motivate them. It might seem counter-intuitive, but when they do well, that's when you give them more challenges. And, believe it or not, that's a reward!

It never ceases to amaze me how many people react so positively to challenge. You would think that giving people hard things to do would put them off, but no—it galvanizes their resolve and spurs them on to even greater heights.

I once climbed a small mountain. OK, just a big, somewhat steep hill. The point is that I would see the summit ahead, make my way there, pat myself on the back, and then look up and realize it wasn't the ultimate summit. There was another summit above me. Up I went again: same result, same false summit.

There's something instinctive about climbing, about wanting to prove to ourselves and others that we are capable of tackling the challenges we are presented with. So many times in my career I have been surprised by what people achieved when they put their minds to it. They reached goals I didn't think they could reach. I think they achieved things *they* didn't think they could do—at the start.

The effect on me was pronounced. I began giving difficult challenges to people who others in senior management thought were incapable of accomplishing them. I once handed the Marketing department to a smart woman who had been a customer service and claims manager. She had no experience in marketing but was intelligent, logical, good with data. And when I gave her some of my marketing interview questions, she did better than most marketing professionals I'd interviewed! Maybe she accepted the role because she didn't realize what she was getting into. And maybe that naïveté was key to her success. She just went out and climbed the mountain. She never knew that she couldn't climb that mountain.

The same is true of many people who started businesses within the Admiral Group. I went out specifically to hire really talented people, not necessarily people with a lot of relevant experience.

And then I gave those people the ball and said, "Get on with it." And they did. To my credit, most of the time, those people rose up as I had suspected they would and they conquered the challenges in front of them, achieving far more than they thought they could. What individuals can do never ceases to amaze me.

And their reward? You guessed it: another challenge!

One last reward. This is a combination of monetary and spiritual reward: shares in the company.

Today almost every member of staff in Admiral has shares in the business. We give shares, over time, to all staff, no matter what job they have. Everyone. Why? Simply put, we want our staff to feel like they own a part of the company. And the best way to achieve that? Give them part of the company to own!

Staff ownership in Admiral goes back to before the beginning, when I negotiated shares for myself and my management team. We then went through those years of threats, deceit, lawyers, etc., which resulted in the validation of the value of our shares. We took our "capital-light" business model to the ultimate parent in Bermuda, but they said we "weren't core." (I've told many people over many years, never tell me that something "isn't core." This was why!) At the time this was a bit of a blow, but today I can only say "Thank you!" As already noted (no harm in saying this twice!), today Admiral has a value of £9 billion and has paid well over £3 billion in dividends since 1999. But hey, we weren't core.

We got lucky and found one guy in one venture capital (VC) firm who was willing to listen, understand, and appreciate a pretty unique insurance business. If we hadn't met Owen Clarke when we did, I don't know what would have happened to us. Owen's patience and perceptiveness paid off in the best deal his firm ever did. Owen and his firm deserve every penny because he took the time to understand the reinsurance model when no one else would—and then convince the powers that be in his organization that we were worth backing.

By the way, the reinsurers have also done quite well, as Admiral's results have been pretty brilliant since 2000. In particular, Munich Re did very long-term deals with us, taking a punt on our future when it wasn't obvious to do so. Munich Re also picked up a substantial shareholding in 2002, which has also been incredibly remunerative for them. They too deserve every penny they've made with us because when they got involved on January 1, 2000 success was far from certain.

The point: We went from being a fairly typical company where just managers had an ownership interest to one where all staff had an ownership interest.

Why did we extend the ownership beyond managers, giving away shares we could have kept for ourselves? When we did the deal with Owen and the VC firm, we only knew one thing for sure: There was another transaction coming.

Arithmetic is fun!

Once a year, from the beginning of 2000 until float, we gave out units in the staff trust. Everyone got some, but good performers and those who were with us longer got more. When we floated, everyone was ready to calculate what their shares would be worth. When we announced that the float value would be £2.75 per share, and we explained the conversion rate of old units to new shares, the arithmetic commenced.

One young woman in our document services area had been with us since the mid-90s. She did her calculation and turned to her manager and said, "Wow, this is fantastic, I'm going to get £3,600! I can take a holiday!" Her manager, knowing how long she'd been with us, was puzzled. He looked at the paper with her calculations and smiled. "It's not £3,600, it's £36,000!" She fell over. She heard the words and she fainted!

THE POWER OF APPRECIATION

Owen and his team were very upfront, telling us they generally held companies for three to five years, possibly stretching it to six or seven if absolutely needed. From Day 1 of our new lives we heard the clock ticking.

At that time, late 1999, we weren't thinking that someday we'd become a public company. We thought the most likely exit for the VC would be a trade sale. We knew that if that happened the managers, who were rolling their old equity into the new, VC-backed venture, would do fine. Even if our business was sold for a low value, we'd all be millionaires.

But, we reasoned, if the company was sold to a competitor it was likely that the competitor would consolidate operations. Maybe they'd leave Cardiff open for sales but close the Swansea office and move customer service to their center in Upper Somewhereelseham. Probably slim down our IT department because most of that would be done centrally, etc. So in the event of a sale, not only would our staff not get any benefit, many of them would likely lose their jobs.

We didn't think that was fair.

The VC had offered us additional shares for managers. We took those additional shares and created a staff trust. I think they gave us 10 percent (this was on top of what shareholder managers had rolled over). When we told them that we wanted to use 2 percent for managers and 8 percent for all other staff, they paused. They explained that usually shares were just for senior managers. But hey, they added, if we wanted to distribute them to all of our staff, that was OK with them. They were amazingly open-minded.

When we floated the business in September 2004, some 1,400 members of staff split up nearly £60 million ($100 million in the day). Our flotation did wonders for the quality of the vehicles in the car park!

Post-float, Admiral continued with share ownership for all. We made sure in the float to have shareholders approve that we could distribute up to 10 percent of the company over 10 years to all staff. At current value that means we're distributing some £900 million over 10 years. Trust me, if you walk down any corridor in Admiral and ask out loud "What's the share price?" someone will respond very quickly with the right answer!

Does it work? Does Admiral get more bang for its buck because of share ownership for all? I think yes. I have seen people care a little more for the customers, work a bit harder to save money, and be generally engaged in what is going on because of share ownership.

Then there's the pride. The pride in knowing that their friends work for companies that don't give shares. The pride in knowing that every time we announce our dividend they are going to get some. The pride in sharing in the success on those days when the shares rise or hit new highs. And the managers who gave up additional shares that went to all staff, how did they do? Millionaires all. I believe that spreading the wealth made everyone wealthier.

Just about everybody has targets. Can you hit your targets yourself? No. Would you like it if your people, the ones who will hit those targets, were more energized, more motivated, more inspired all day, every day? There are many ways to achieve this, not least of which are the rewards discussed above. But there's more. This is where it gets fun.

PILLAR 4: FUN

CHAPTER 9

LET THE GAMES BEGIN!

Have you noticed? All of these pillars of Admiral culture that we've covered support the main point of this book, and of my management philosophy. At the risk of mixing architectural metaphors, you might call the following sentence the foundation of my philosophy: If people like what they do, they'll do it better.

We communicate, we treat each other as equals, and we are fairly rewarded—that's why we like it here. And, oh yeah: We have fun, don't we?

This isn't altruism. All of this is aimed at giving Admiral a competitive advantage via its people. It's not about hiring more of them or paying exorbitant salaries, especially because there are more than 10,000 people in the Admiral Group. We want to have a competitive advantage via people because we work smarter, harder, and better.

Many years ago, in Admiral's early days, I had an office (shame!) and I was sitting at my desk, working as I sometimes did, when I heard a few people laughing. I paused. More laughter. Now I started to pay attention. A pause followed by more, even louder laughter—clearly a bunch of people, not just one or two. "Well," I thought, "this has gone on long enough, I have to go out there and tell them to get back to work." More laughter. I weighed my options. Maybe I'll just stand in front of these people and cross my arms; they'd get the message. Hey, I was the boss, right? I pushed my chair back, got up, and made a move for the door.

More laughter. I stopped. I thought. Wait a minute, what could be better than a bunch of people feeling comfortable enough to have a laugh in the office?

In that instant I realized that this was not something I should worry about and stamp out—it was something I should be pleased about and encourage! I have never again thought of stopping anyone from having a laugh in the office. If anything, I'll go over to them and join in.

I had learned the value of humor and entertainment at work already—not at INSEAD, but when I worked for Herb in Chicago. As I grew in the early days of Admiral, I started to think more about this. Why don't we have fun at the office every day? We can still work hard, but certainly inside a nine-hour workday we can find a few minutes to have a laugh, right?

To officially endorse this doctrine we created the Ministry of Fun (MoF). This gave it the prominence it deserved, so everyone would pay attention. We were serious about fun: We wanted to always have something going on so that everyone would have a good time at work.

Each month a different department is in charge of the MoF. It's on the calendar so events are planned well in advance. There's a small budget for props and prizes, but nothing extravagant. This isn't about someone winning an all-expenses-paid holiday but rather about all staff having a few minutes two or three times a week to relax and de-stress.

Memorable MoF events included armchair Olympics, pancake races (careful, we had a few injuries), egg roulette, soak-a-manager, balloon release, cake baking, picture competitions, office golf, karaoke, video games, table tennis, dressing up your manager… the list goes on and on—we have a creative staff! And this doesn't even include big events, like Admiral's Got Talent.

One of my favorites was the closing-door race. The doors at the ends of the lift lobbies closed and locked automatically. So, how far away could someone be for them to start moving as the door begins to shut and still reach it before it closes? The door would be held open, and the contestant would stand as far away as he or she thought practical. On "Go!" the door was let go and the contestant would walk really fast to see if they could get to the door before it closed. Some impressive distances were covered. If only we could encourage everyone to walk with such purpose every day!

Laughing and staffing

Here's one fun-related measurement: staff retention. A miserable worker is likely to be looking for another job. Who is more valuable: someone with two years' experience or someone who has been with you 90 days? The value of experience cannot be underestimated. If you can keep people in your organization, especially if it is growing, that's a good thing. If a little fun along the way reduces attrition, you'll boost efficiency and, at the end of the day, the bottom line.

PHILOSOPHY

We made some goofs. One time the underwriting department offered a quiz. Hey-ho—they really took the bit between their teeth and put out a 200-question quiz. The entire IT department closed down for the afternoon to complete it! Whoops.

Sometimes participation flagged. But we asked around and found that almost everyone liked just knowing there were things going on, even if they didn't get involved. Some people would come to me, frustrated, wondering why an event was proceeding with so few people involved. I'd say, "Stay with it." The very fact that we do these things helps everyone and boosts their opinion of working at Admiral. Having fun isn't in any way limited to the MoF. In every team there are no real restrictions on ways they can have fun. So you'll often see small groups of people in Admiral adding up points from this or that, or doing something a bit odd as part of a team game. This applies to all departments. There's no reason that teams in IT can't have as much fun as teams in Sales.

Just as a reminder: All of this fun is ultimately aimed at a better economic result. Because by making Admiral a place people like, they'll do better work.

This isn't brain surgery. What do you really want? You want your team, department, company to be mind-bogglingly successful. What I saw throughout my career was that fear and intimidation might be able to get some people to do great things in short bursts. But over time, such a style works against productivity and innovation. So, I turned in the other direction.

Think of your own experiences. As I asked before, when did you really do your best work? When you were being forced or when you wanted to do something? Did you find yourself working a bit harder, a bit smarter, when you really liked what you were doing? Maybe it was cooking, maybe it was writing an essay, maybe it was flying a kite, maybe it was even working(!). Whatever it was, take a look at your relationship with that event and how you performed.

You likely do your best work when you want to do something. There you go. Maybe this entire manual can be summed up in these sentences. If we can get everyone excited about coming to work, then we can generate more energy, more thought, and more care from them. And that energy, thought, and care will give us a much better chance at success. In Admiral's case I believe it has given Admiral a sustainable competitive advantage.

Please don't make the mistake of thinking that fun is something separate from the business. Fun is part of the business and should be measured. Admiral isn't about having fun just because we're nice people (though we are!). Admiral is on about fun because we believe we will get a better result if people are happy in their work. Everything you do in business should be measured. If a measurement doesn't come out positive, ask yourself why you are doing it (more on this later). Many things are easy to measure. You run an advertisement and you measure the response and then decide whether the cost of running that advertisement was worth it. Well, fun is no different. It's just a bit harder to measure.

For example, for years Admiral sponsored the jerseys of the Wales rugby team, the national team of the national sport. We knew going in that we would never get enough new car insurance business to justify this expense. So why did we do it? Before we committed to the sponsorship, we polled staff and found that they were in favor. In fact, we offered them a choice of a bonus of £20 each or having the Admiral name on the country's jerseys.

They voted for the jerseys. We knew that having our name on the jerseys would be a source of pride for our workforce. The value of this pride? Dunno. As much as the cost of the sponsorship? We thought so, and so we sponsored the team for seven years. When it came time to renew for the fourth time, the cost had gone up to a point where we decided that we'd have to find less expensive ways to generate that pride. There's always a point where a cost is too great for the benefit. Pride is a tough thing to measure. We know that staff loved seeing Admiral on the jerseys: their team, their country. What could be better?

So measure as best you can, even if sometimes the measurement tools are inexact. The perfect is the enemy of the good and you can often expend far too much resource trying to be exact than in just making a decision based on a reasonable amount of information.

Fun is part of the reason (one entire pillar's worth) why staff think we're one of the best places to work. They don't always see the relationship between our financial success and being one of the World's Best Places to Work (14th at last count). These are not two disparate things. We are a financial success in part because we're a Great Place to Work. One helped cause the other, which in turn helps cause the other, which helps… voilà, another virtuous circle!

Here's another thing about fun: why not? One time I was working in Chicago and I really disliked the job. I would walk some 25 minutes to work, and by the time I'd reached the office door I could feel my teeth clenching in the back of my mouth—and I hadn't even entered the office yet! I said to myself then: If I can at all help it I'll never work where I dislike it again. I left that job shortly thereafter and every time I worked where I didn't like it, I left as quickly as was practical.

If you've worked in a job you really didn't like, did you find you could go home every evening and, just like flicking a light switch, be a happy camper at home? I've worked in places that made me miserable. It took a long time to unwind at home, and sometimes wasn't possible at all. Often I couldn't even find the switch to flick, much less flick it!

It's bad enough that some employers ruin your day at work, but ruining your time at home should not be tolerated. If people lighten up a bit, have a bit of fun during the day, and know that their boss and workday is not a non-stop stress event, then it's much easier to have a nice home life as well. And we're back to virtuous circles...

Fun stuff

✓ Laughter is a good thing.
✓ Be serious about fun.
✓ Let loose your staff's creativity.
✓ Fun = happiness = profit.
✓ Less stress at work means less stress at home.
✓ Happy employees stick around.

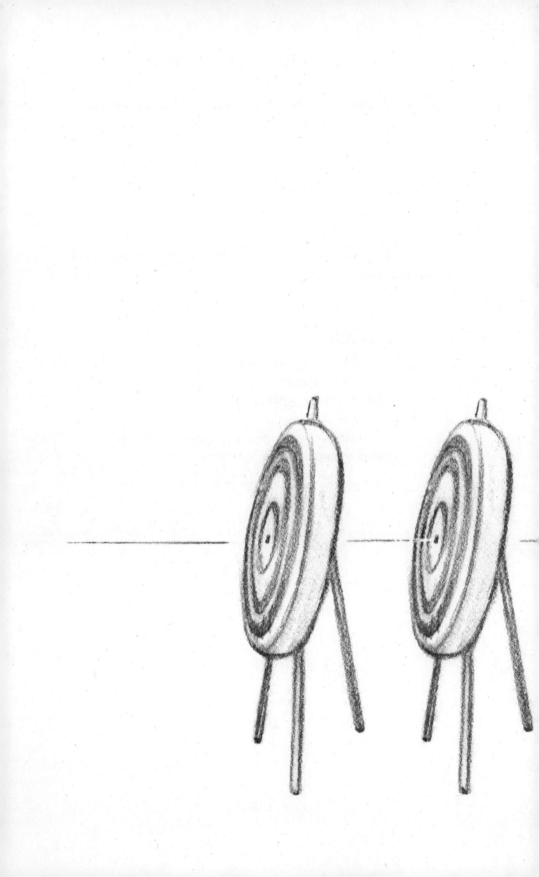

PART 3

THE THREE KEYS TO SUCCESS

Now that you've heard my story, learned a bit about the company history, and had a dose of philosophy that guides the management style at Admiral, let's get real.

It's time to discuss the nuts and bolts of management and leadership. To think specifically about how to build a team, motivate them, earn their respect, and, most of all, get great results. As you read about the challenges depicted in these chapters, think (there's that word again) about how you, as a leader, might handle them.

Now grab a pen. Reflect on great leaders you've worked with in your past. (If you've had any, that is.) What made them great? What about poor leaders? What made them poor?

Think about all the people who have led you over time—teachers, bosses, friends, coaches, whoever. Write down the characteristics that made the good ones good and the bad ones bad.

But as you jot down your lists, try to focus on how those leaders affected you and your life. Think more about their interactions with you than their general demeanor and performance.

We know that management isn't a science and there is no formula for success. So, the best place to start is with yourself: What do you like? What do you dislike? It may not be the perfect guide, but it's a great place to start.

I've made my lists. Please finish yours before continuing on to read mine.

Lousy leaders:

- Didn't listen
- Had big egos
- Showed little or no appreciation (except for themselves!)
- Didn't connect with me
- Stifled innovation and initiative
- Cared little for my future
- Weren't trustworthy
- Were hypocritical
- Kept changing their minds about things
- Kept to their ideas even with evidence to the contrary

Great leaders:

- Boosted my confidence
- Encouraged creative thinking
- Let me do things
- Appreciated my efforts
- Trusted me
- Included me in decision-making

When I'm asked what would make someone who reports to me a great leader, one of the first things I tell them is that a great leader destroys her or his targets. It's not about trust or appreciation or inspiration. It's about the targets. Great leaders don't meet targets, they destroy targets; they deliver results that are far better than anyone expects.

So here we have the taffy pull of leadership. On the one side is your team, looking for inspiration, responsibility, inclusiveness, help, friendliness, and encouragement. And on the other side you've got a demand for results.

Wait a minute. Actually, it isn't a taffy pull at all. Very simply: If you can satisfy the people you lead then you have a much improved chance of satisfying those people leading you. (Of course, it helps to have good people to start with, but the recruitment chapter is yet to come.)

As you review your past supervisors and ponder your own leadership style, keep this seemingly stupid but incredibly important question in mind: Can you hit your targets yourself?

Of course not! You need your team—and you will have to do a great job motivating them.

As CEO, my most important task was to ensure that the right people were in the right positions, that they had the tools they needed, and that they were all highly motivated. Same goes for you.

Every morning I reminded myself: This is about them. I had emails waiting, meetings scheduled, decisions looming. But I focused first on the people I had contact with. Were they happy? Motivated? Were they motivating the people under them?

That motivating begins with a "Good morning," as mentioned earlier. Of course, you have your own work to do. But your people come first. Why? Simple: because without them you will not hit your targets.

As I walked into the office each morning, I made sure I was thinking about the people around me. During my time at Elephant in the US, the distance from the lift to my desk could be covered in 10 seconds. But if I went through a different set of doors from the lift lobby, it'd take me three minutes. And all along the way

I'd be greeting people, saying hello, asking how they were doing, what they were up to, commenting on the weather (almost always nice!), etc. What a valuable use of two minutes, 50 seconds!

Remember, as I mentioned earlier, you are incredibly important to the people you manage. Just saying "hello" to someone can make their day, while ignoring someone can ruin their day.

Three keys to being a *great* manager

I've worked hard to distill the qualities needed for great leadership and management. I want to keep it simple, so that everyone can see that great leadership and management are not as difficult to achieve as one might be led to believe. I've landed on three things that can help you become a great leader or manager:

1. Make great decisions.
2. Be great with people.
3. Be creative and innovative.

The next three chapters look at these three things in more detail. They are *really* important. When I do management talks I almost invariably start by talking about these three keys to success.

CHAPTER 10

DECISIVE MOMENTS

As a leader you make decisions all the time: big ones and small ones and everything in between. There are of course many aspects to your job: planning, motivation, analysis, creative thinking. But what you're really paid to do is hit your targets (blow them away?) and to do that you have to make decisions.

So wouldn't it be nice to make good decisions? I see four aspects to achieving this:

1. Data.
2. The Team, the Team, the Team.
3. Keep the Earth in the window.
4. Make the decision.

Data comes in all shapes and sizes. It can be a quantitative study of statistical significance carried out by a reputable organisation and flowed into a spreadsheet. Data can also be what your gut tells you. Your gut isn't stupid; it is based on data. On many occasions I've seen two very clever people look at the same data, reach radically different conclusions, and propose very different ways forward. There must be more to data than just figures on a page. I suggest recruiting more guts.

Once you verify the data you need to interrogate it—that is, investigate to understand what the data is saying. It's a bit like listening to a dog barking. It is unlikely that you are fluent in dog, so you try to understand. Does it need to pee? Is there an intruder? Does it want that cake on your plate? You gesture to the door, look around for an intruder, hold the plate up. Or if you've had the dog for years, you know instinctively. You can usually figure it out, though it can get tricky.

Data is similar. It just sits there, waiting for you to figure out what it means. Look at the chart below. To practice your data interrogation skills, you can take pretty much any chart, preferably on a subject you know nothing about, and ask a bunch of questions that would help you figure out what you're looking at.

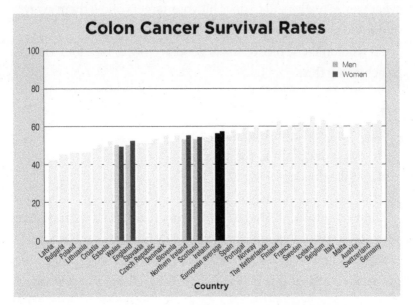

DECISIVE MOMENTS

The first chart shows colon cancer survival rates. As you can see, Wales and England are below the European average and well below the best-performing country, Germany. The jump-to conclusion is that Germany is better at handling colon cancer than they are in the UK. And that might be right. But before I jump to that conclusion, I'd like to know a few things.

What's the first thing I look at? It's the axes. I want to know what is being measured on each axis, and what is the scale?

We'll come back to colon cancer in a minute, but first, look at the second and third charts. The left one is from one of our offices showing sales conversion on the phones over the course of a year. When you look at that line you think: "Wow, nice move!"

The other chart doesn't look much like progress, does it? But both charts are pictures of the exact same data. The only difference is the scale. If I want to present numbers that look quite good, I show the first chart. If I want to show numbers that look like little progress has been made, I show the second chart.

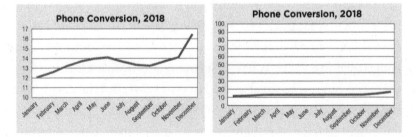

Now take another look at the colon cancer chart. First is the Y axis—so we know it's showing "relative survival" in percentages. We can interrogate that later, but for now you know it's about surviving colon cancer—not how many people get it, not how many cases are detected. It's something about surviving colon cancer. The X axis is just the list of countries; simple.

Now then, what are some of your questions?

I'd want to know how many cases are in the data set. It's not shown here. In essence, how sensitive is the data to a small move in numbers? If we had 10 more successes over five years in Wales would we be up with Scotland or still behind England? We don't know.

Second, are we sure all countries define colon cancer in exactly the same way? Perhaps some cases of colon cancer get registered as stomach cancer, and the survival rates for stomach cancer show Germany in a very different light. We don't know just from the chart provided.

Third, when do they identify colon cancer? Perhaps in Germany they pick it up earlier when it's more treatable. Which might mean that it's not the relative quality of the care that differs but rather the disease detection that makes the difference. This could be key if you are a government minister about to allocate £100 million towards treating colon cancer. Do you apply it to the treatment or do you apply it to the detection? If you were spending that kind of money wouldn't you want to make sure you really understood what this chart was saying before you allocated your spend? Is Germany really the model that should be followed? The data is over five years. What if Germany was brilliant three to five years ago but not so great in the last two years, but the data is not weighted by recent performance? When you interrogate the data you might find that Germany really is far ahead of other countries in colon cancer cure, but you need to work a bit harder before you can make that call (and spend £100 million!).

Here's something I'd recommend: Keep your own data and charts. Don't farm out to a subordinate the data collection or chart making. Do it yourself. You'll get a lot more from it. My archived files are full of spreadsheets tracking weekly calls into every part of Admiral since the very beginning of Admiral time.

By dropping those figures into the spreadsheet each week, I got to know the patterns well. I knew immediately, intuitively, if things were getting better or worse. (Or when I needed to check the data source!) When I saw deviations from the norm, I started asking questions. My spreadsheets grew and grew as I thought of how to measure data against different things. Because I was looking at the data myself, regularly, I was able to ask more questions, better questions. I'd add information and eliminate now-useless info, and get the answers quickly.

For many years I kept a chart of monthly quotes done by Admiral through each of the four big price comparison firms. After a while I added the percentage of price comparison sales for each supplier, and then I added marketing spend, and then I compared it to quotes, percentage, and marketing spend from the previous year. And then I looked at a rolling three-month ad spend and then added a rolling 12-month ad spend and then a percentage of the total spend of the four companies and then... you can see where this is going.

By doing the spreadsheet myself I was able to get my hands dirty with the data and ask all sorts of interesting questions. Over time some of the questions and comparisons I was making at the beginning were no longer relevant, so I stopped recording data for those and kept on with the others.

If you keep the spreadsheets yourself, you gain a deep understanding of the numbers. Many of your competitors are looking at monthly or quarterly reports with built-in disadvantages. Namely:

These leaders are disconnected. The information is prepared by someone else. You may not even know who prepared it.

The information is late, coming weeks after the last data point is collected.

The leaders' responses are sluggish. It takes time to respond to questions or requests for more data. Replies come only after additional weeks have slipped by. It might be months before you're in a position to make a decision or change.

Sorry, way too slow. Keep at least some of the data yourself. That way, just as you quickly understand your dog's bark, you'll know what the numbers are trying to tell you. Keeping and knowing your own data means you make better arguments when needed. You'll sound confident of the numbers and their meaning. For a pretty simple reason: you are.

Too many people think that when they become a manager they have to be Superwoman or Superman. They have to make all the decisions on their own, lest others think they are weak and ineffective managers. The "buck stops here" mentality.

Nothing could be further from the truth at Admiral. The best managers use as many people as they can to help them do their job well. They are open and honest about what they're good at and not so good at, what they know and what they don't, and where and when they need help.

Sadly, I have yet to meet Superwoman or Superman. The best leaders first realise that it's the result that matters, and it doesn't matter how many other people help produce it. Then they realise that using other people to get that result is a skill in itself.

To be a successful manager you have to have some ego, for sure. But it's managing that ego and not being too proud to ask for assistance that helps make good people great.

If you're human (and not from the planet Krypton), you have good days and bad days. Let people know. Remember, you can almost never over-communicate!

I used to have a Mood Meter on my wall. It was a lovely framed print of a golf hole. I rolled up some Blu Tack to act as the ball. When you saw the ball next to the flag, you knew I was in a good mood. If the ball was on the green, but a fair distance from the flag, things were OK. If the ball was in the sand trap, watch out. And if you ever came in and saw the ball in the water, turn around and try another day!

It's not like I jumped up every 15 minutes to move the ball. It was there symbolically to let people know that I too have good days and bad days. It was there to tell people that I'm going to do my best to be positive and welcoming, but sometimes...

Trust is an essential part of leadership. You want people to follow you, even if they don't know precisely where you're taking them. To get them to follow you they have to trust you, both personally and professionally.

So be sure to use other people to help you make decisions. To get people to open up, you have to open up. To help you with decisions, they have to trust you. Earn that trust by being honest with them, even when you're not feeling 100 percent.

Members of your team may provide different bits of data. Your role is to synthesize that information, gather opinions and choose the way forward. The more opinions you gather, the better your decision-making is likely to be.

Sometimes you just need one or two people to give their thoughts, or perhaps that's all you have time for. Sometimes you need as many opinions as you can get. And yes, sometimes you get so many different thoughts that you can't see the forest for the trees. But that just shows how difficult making such a decision would have been on your own.

To make good decisions you have to know your perspective. At every level of management that perspective gets wider and longer.

I learned to drive when I was 15 years old and got my license the day after my 16th birthday. Having been a few decades in the car insurance business, this scares the bejeezus out of me now!

THE THREE KEYS TO SUCCESS

My driving instructor, Mr Little (still remember his name!), made a big impression on me. He taught me something that also applies to business: "high-aim steering." Mr Little told me to keep my eyes up. If I just looked at the bumper of the car in front of me, he explained, all I'd see would be what's in between my eyes and that bumper. But if I lifted my eyes and looked well into the distance, maybe a light or two ahead, I could see so much more—including that bumper in front of me—and drive more safely.

High-aim steering applies to management. A team manager is concerned with hitting daily and weekly targets and should keep his or her eyes focused on these. The next level of management should probably be looking at monthly and annual targets. As you go higher up in management you need to be looking further into the distance—while taking in everything in the short term as well. The CEO has to be thinking, "How are we going to do in 10 years' time and what do I need to do today to help meet those goals?"

This is a pretty big challenge. Who knows what the world will be like in 10 years' time? The Covid-19 pandemic brought that lesson home. The only thing we know for sure? It won't be like it is today.

There's a version of high-aim steering that's, well, extremely high. When I coach senior managers, I tell them to put the Earth in the window.

Ever see the film *Apollo 13*? Great movie. Tom Hanks, Bill Paxton, Kevin Bacon, directed by Ron Howard. If you haven't seen it, see it. If you have seen it, maybe you remember the scene where they have to fire the engine propelling their spacecraft while keeping it aligned properly for re-entry into the Earth's atmosphere. A mistake would mean incineration.

Commander Jim Lovell (that's Tom) doesn't have the electronics that would normally guide the ship. But he does have a little window and knows that if they can steady the craft well enough to keep the Earth in that window as the engine fires, they'll be heading in the right direction. (Bonus tip: Hanks says, "It's going to take all three of us." The Team, the Team, the Team.)

It's the same for management decision-making, hopefully minus the potential incineration. Just keep the Earth in the window. Keep your big-picture goals in your line of sight when you make your day-to-day decisions. It'll keep you pointed at that long-term target.

Here's a lesson I learned at INSEAD, but outside the classroom—literally. The sidewalk from a campus coffee spot to a building entrance formed a sensible "L" alongside the buildings and around a grassy area. I couldn't help but notice the well-worn diagonal path through the grass—the direct route favoured by us busy students.

Ever since, I've applied that lesson to management: Watch where people walk before laying down the sidewalks. That is, watch what people do before creating your rules. Very often, rules are set up by managers who are convinced they're right and believe they know how people will react to those rules. But people often don't do as you've hoped or expected.

Consider the Covid-19 crisis, when at first everyone in Admiral worked from home. As the crisis eased, managers planned a gradual return to the office.

Many people, it turned out, preferred to work from home, and many were more productive there. Another consideration: How to maintain social distancing if everyone returned at once. One manager asked me what I thought—impose two days in the office and three at home, or three in the office and two at home?

"Hang on," I said. "Before you lay down those sidewalks, look where people are walking." I suggested he send around a sign-up sheet with no requirements, and see how many days each wants to come in? When you see the results, you'll know if your team wants to come back two or three days a week (or more or less!). Then set your new rules.

Instead of imposing your will, you've made an informed decision. Your team are more likely to be happy with a policy that they helped form. I learned later that landscape architects have a name for those shortcuts through the grass: "desire lines" or "desire paths." Often it helps to listen to others' desires.

Here's a quick story about listening to your gut, keeping the Earth in the window, and getting help with a decision. It's also about crime and the FBI and includes a chase scene. Who says business is boring?

When I was working in futures brokerage in Chicago, I had made my way up to senior vice president, managing marketing and sales in a new organisation that was still finding its feet. One day I got a call from someone I didn't know who said he could deliver the entire customer list of one of our competitors. Strange. My gut reactions: shock, skepticism, and apprehension. But I played along and told him I'd get back to him.

I sat back and thought about this, knowing how wrong it was and how bad it would be if such a transaction were tied to our company. But I wanted to find out more. I called the guy back and got him to tell me which company, how many customers, and what they might cost to buy. It quickly became evident we weren't dealing with professionals. He was selling the list for $15,000.

I knew what it would cost to advertise for those customers: The "real" price would have been closer to $1 million. (This was in the early 1980s.)

What to do? I went to see Herb, my boss, for advice. He too was shocked and said we should contact the FBI. So we did. The FBI asked me to play along and see what this was all about.

I had a couple more conversations with the guy who, it became apparent, was quite young. I pressed him on how he came to have this information and he said he worked in the other company's data room.

The FBI said we should play it out. I told the guy that a friend of mine would meet him in a crowded spot in Chicago. He should bring the data and my friend would have the money. I told him I couldn't be there because I couldn't be seen to be involved if this somehow got out.

What the kid didn't know was that my "friend" was an FBI agent. What the FBI didn't know was that this kid was a cross-country champion!

The sting was going as planned but at the last minute the kid smelled it and took off down LaSalle Street in the heart of Chicago's business district, running full speed. The FBI agents gave chase but quickly realised they were not going to catch him. They yelled that they were federal agents, and he finally did something intelligent—stopped running and gave himself up. (He was just a kid working part-time in the data room, trying to make a quick buck. He got a suspended sentence and I never heard from or about him again.)

OK, maybe my decision was the obvious one. But any of us can face temptation. That data would have been very valuable to our firm and me. But I listened to my gut: Do the right thing.

In a way, I kept the Earth in the window: the long-term reputation of our new company. It was certainly not worth the risk of short-term, ill-gotten gains. And I enlisted the help of Herb to confirm my gut reaction. Right decision, good story. The exciting chase through downtown Chicago was just a bonus.

Don't get me wrong, I have a very clear sense of winning and I always want to win (second best is not the best!), but I want to win the right way. I don't want to win by cheating. I don't want to win by taking shortcuts. This was wrong and had to be stopped.

Is it lonely at the top? Sometimes. Especially at decision time.

As you know, I constantly preach the Team, the Team, the Team. Few, if any, decisions should be taken on your own. So how can it be lonely at the top if the summit is crowded with teammates?

But that's not right. It can be a lonely feeling because the responsibility for decisions rests with you. Once you make a decision you cannot blame others if things don't work. Yes, extenuating circumstances can lead you to bad decisions, but when you are called upon to explain a failure, it doesn't look favourably on you to say, "It was somebody else's fault." The final call comes from you.

This can create tension within a management team. Let's say your marketing manager brings you a creative treatment that you don't think will work. The manager has studies and numbers to support her treatment but you are unconvinced.

First you try to influence her. Perhaps you call in others to see if they can convince her—or perhaps they can help convince you. For the sake of this example, let's say this step just muddies the water; no clear outcome.

This decision puts you in a bind: Do you let your marketing

manager do her job and run with her treatment or do you put your foot down and insist she does it your way?

There are arguments on each side. But you must remember, if things don't work you cannot go to your boss and say, "Well, I knew it wouldn't work but Mary-Anne thought it would and so we did it her way. She's to blame." If you decide to do it Mary-Anne's way then you have to be behind the decision, even if you're not! If you feel that strongly about a choice—that you could not justify it to your superior in the event of failure—then you should step in before the decision is made and ensure a decision that you can support is taken.

These are not easy decisions. In many instances you might think you're right, but you know that you don't know—you can't know—for certain. You know that it's possible that Mary-Anne might be right.

This is where it gets lonely. You either support a decision you don't have full confidence in (but might have to express confidence in later) or overrule a colleague (and probably demotivate her).

You could try to find a compromise; many excellent solutions are found that way. But compromises sometimes lead to poor results, when either of the two things being compromised would have done better!

One time I was working on an ad idea for one of our price comparison businesses. I gave them my vision for the ad. But I couldn't be on site to see it through and left it to them to interpret my vision. The result was awful. We tried to fix it before it went out but, again, using compromise—one thought from one person, another idea from somewhere else and a third from across the pond—probably only made it worse. We did run it—for about three days. Results were poor and we all, mercifully, agreed to kill it, bury it, and never talk about it again. Ouch.

How do you deal with loneliness at the top? All I can suggest is that you remind yourself of your purpose and realise that this is part of the job. Everybody needs motivation, even those at the top. When you're at the top, you have to harness this need and remind yourself that you will get a lot of glory when things go well.

You will spend much of your time as a manager weighing arguments. But don't spend too much time. The only way to make a good decision is this: Make a decision. Indecision is a bad decision. A good leader does whatever he or she thinks reasonable but realises that a decision needs to be made. And once that decision is made you move on to the next. Decision-making shouldn't have four stomachs; don't chew the cud of decision-making.

Of course you need to review your decisions later to see if you are making good calls or not and to try to evaluate your decision-making process, but once you make the call, move on. So many leaders are ineffectual because they never really make the decision. Either they constantly request more information—then more and more and more—or they sort of reach a conclusion and then hesitate, and change things a bit, tinker here and there and then, wow, maybe it's time for more information. It's not good for the morale of the team to leave a decision hanging.

You must assess the risks of all your choices. In car insurance we're used to thinking in terms of "frequency and severity." This type of analysis comes in handy for all sorts of decision-making in virtually every business. When you're trying to assess the risks (after all, that's the bulk of decision-making), one has a choice of one set of risks over another. You are looking for and assessing the probability of something going awry, as well as the damage if it did go wrong, versus the benefit if things went right. Is the upside potential worth the downside risk?

DECISIVE MOMENTS

Let's say you're on holiday and a helicopter ride is offered. Do you go or not? The person extending the offer senses your concern about safety. He says, "In this part of the world you are far less likely to be in a helicopter crash than you are to get hit with a coconut." There's one easy decision—don't sit under a coconut tree! But that's just frequency. But you—being a canny insurance person—reason that few people survive a helicopter crash, while most people survive a coconut attack.

Helicopters are a classic risk example of low frequency, high severity. It's unlikely to go bad on you—but if it does, it's likely to be catastrophic. In business you are looking at these types of decisions all the time.

Two tips: 1) Test first if possible, which provides more data, arguably very good data, thus reducing the risk; 2) try to ensure there's a back door to undo your decision if it doesn't look like it's working.

As a manager you have to balance need for information with making a decision. One of the best things I ever learned as a leader was the simple saying: The perfect is the enemy of the good. I have seen too many good managers try to create "perfect" tests before making decisions and, as such, expend way too much time and effort (and usually money, too) in making said decision.

So try to set up the simplest, quickest test possible. This might mean not using IT at all. Maybe you get people to put ticks on a piece of paper that you pick up every evening. Simple: Gather the team and gauge the collective gut.

One business I'm involved in normally sells its product b2b. But it wanted to test a b2c offering. I suggested that it take the lowest possible sale price the business could live with and do a small test on that. Why? Because if it didn't work at the lowest possible price, then you can forget it. No further testing needed. But if it works at the low price, higher prices can be tested in the future.

With these simple tests you are looking for clear signals—very black or very white. If it's grey, fair enough, you might need to do a more detailed test or find other ways to get information. But if it's blindingly clear then you'll know quickly whether or not you should proceed.

Design your test to show something simple that will give you a basic reading. Don't spend a lot of money or time looking for a result to the third decimal point. And do this first test quickly as well—project momentum is important. Long tests can be draining.

And that back door I mentioned? Make sure it's unlocked. If things don't turn out as you planned, you need to be able to scoot out. Usually that's easy, but not always. Property decisions, for instance, often lock you into long-term leases or obligations. The more accessible the back door, the less work you need to do up front. Correspondingly, the smaller that back door, the more effort you need to put in up front to make sure the decision is the right one. For property decisions, this means trying to get exit options every five years or, at a minimum, the right to sublet. Something that might help you if the future is different from how you anticipate.

When we began the process that led to building Ty Admiral, our headquarters building in Cardiff, we knew that a build like this would lock us into a 20- or 25-year lease. So we examined all the possible alternatives with microscopic attention to make sure that this was going to be the best solution.

We were committing ourselves to a large amount of space for at least two decades. Could we really know in 2013 what our space requirements would be in 2030?

We made our decision but as we progressed the builders gave us an option to build an additional floor at a reasonable cost. We knew we'd be taking up two-thirds of the space the day we moved in but we felt the future was a bit uncertain—we might never fill up the rest of the space. Taking an additional floor might just be adding empty space.

At first it turned out to be the wrong call. It took less than five years for us to fill Ty Admiral to the brim. We then had to start taking space elsewhere in the city to keep up with our growth. (Ironically, the building we left when we moved to Ty Admiral, and couldn't wait to get out of, is once again home to hundreds of Admiral staff!) But then along came Covid-19. Ty Admiral was virtually closed for more than a year.

Meanwhile, we kitted out almost 10,000 staff to be able to work from home, and many of them loved this. It is unlikely that Admiral will ever go back to asking all staff to come to an office every day. Admiral is likely to go to some sort of hot-desking in its offices. On any given day many staff will be working from home, and that means that Ty Admiral will probably prove to be plenty big.

Deciding factors

✓ Your gut isn't stupid.
✓ But find out what other guts are feeling.
✓ Don't hide your mood. (You can't, anyway.)
✓ The long view matters most.
✓ Pull the damned trigger.

CHAPTER 11

THERE'S NOWT SO QUEER AS FOLK

I have stressed that the number-one ability in a great leader is decision-making, and that to improve your decision-making, you should welcome the input of as many people as is practical. Which leads to my second key to leadership: being *great* with people.

Which in turn leads me to that quaint Yorkshire expression, "There's nowt so queer as folk."

Which summarizes brilliantly the situation surrounding us all: People are weird and they do weird things; live with it.

How do you know if you're a good leader? Simple: People follow you.

How do you know if you're a *great* leader? People follow you over a sustained period of time.

I have seen good leaders who are very introverted. I've seen leaders who are extroverts. I've seen very educated people lead. I've seen uneducated people lead. I don't see that there is much that knits leaders together such that you can create that "leader recipe."

Some people might believe that leaders are born, not made. Not me. Maybe someone's inherent nature at birth plays some part in whether they can become a great leader, but I think just about anyone can succeed at leadership. This is truly a game without rules. So please, don't tell me that you're not the "leader type." If you want to be a good leader, maybe even a *great* leader, I believe you can be. If people follow you, then you're the leader.

I put decision-making at the top of my list of leadership qualities, but it's not the most challenging to achieve. That would be dealing with people, trying to lead them where you want to go. People are complex machines; you need to appeal to them intellectually and emotionally. Having a good balance between the two will help you to be a *great* leader—but a little imbalance can help. Some imbalance may even be necessary because some followers can be led more easily via intellectual links and others through emotional links.

I return to a point I made earlier: What do you stand for?

Answering this question requires a bit of introspection. Who are you—as a person, as a colleague, as a leader? If you were celebrating your 100th birthday and your family put together a book of memories for you, how would you want this sentence completed:

"The people who worked for him found him ....
................"

And this one:

"Her boss said she was the ...."

Happy 100th! But if you're not yet 99 then you might want to give some consideration to how you are going to live up to all those nice things you imagined people would say about you.

Here's another mindset trick to use: The minute you come within a city block of the office, it's showtime! Curtain up! You're on! Leaders are always onstage. They are always being watched, measured, considered, talked about. Everything you do, really everything, makes a difference.

For instance, let's say you got your team together at the end of the day, say seven or eight people, and you want to highlight Sally-Anne's performance that day. What do you need to consider?

Come on, Henry—what could possibly be wrong about giving Sally-Anne a compliment? Aren't leaders supposed to give positive reinforcement? Yes, yes, yes; calm down. I'm not saying that you

The Ministry of Serious Walks

Try this exercise: Get up and walk around as you normally do.

What do you look like to those around you? Do you walk with purpose? Or do you walk like you don't know which way you're going? (Leaders know.) If you walk like you mean it, people will see confidence and take comfort. That means walking with a slight sense of urgency—even if you don't actually know where you're going! Even if you're just headed for the loo.

Watch your posture. Are you upright? Do you look strong or weak? How about approachability? Is your head up—would someone feel comfortable stopping you to ask a question? Or is your head down, and you look completely self-absorbed? Or, worst thing going: walking while looking at your phone. Everything you do is being watched and reviewed. (Nobody said this was fair.)

Remember how important you are to the people you manage. It means you always have to be thinking.

shouldn't pay S-A the compliment. But before you do, think about the other people in the team. Do you really know what goes on in the team? Is it possible that all the other team members think S-A is a lazy, no-good so-and-so and she's pulled the wool over your eyes? Maybe they're thinking that they did everything you are complimenting S-A for, so why don't you compliment them? So, S-A blushes and then rushes home to tell her dog what you said, while others mutter about how unfair you are.

This doesn't mean you don't ever say anything nice about anyone. Or don't speak to anyone at all for fear of troubling someone! You just have to be aware of everyone in the team. Maybe you have to say, 'Sally-Anne did a great job today, as she made two customers cry—from joy at having their problems sorted. I know the rest of you also had a great day satisfying our customers, but I thought it was worth highlighting S-A because so few of our customers cry.'

The next day, look for ways to compliment someone else in the team.

Here's a situation for you. Let's say one of your team members, Diane, is a single mum with two little kids. Immediately, what does that say to you? Right; she is going to have particular needs: school appointments, sick days, and so on. Diane, a good member of the team, comes to you one morning and says, "My little one, Jonny, fell down yesterday and chipped his tooth. The only dentist appointment I could get is this afternoon so I'll have to leave a couple of hours early." She concludes by telling you that there's no possibility of her making up the time.

What do you tell her? Before you answer, tell me what the issues are. What are the things going through your mind that will lead you to your response?

OK, you've listed the issues, now tell me what you'd tell her? (We'll come back to the issues in a minute.)

I suspect most of you would tell Diane, "Fine, take care of your family, that's what's important." I suspect that because you're a nice person who understands the problems single parents have, and why you must help your people, all your people, when they need your help.

Good answer. But the wrong answer.

Now, what did you list for issues? No, the "issues" aren't about being able to cover her work for a couple of hours. That can be done (happens every time she goes on holiday, doesn't it?). The key issue is what the rest of the team is going to think. What is Chris, who doesn't have any family commitments, going to make of this? What stops him from saying, "Hey, I too have to go to the dentist and I'm also leaving at 3 pm and can't make the time up. Ta-ta!"

So, what's the solution?

Well, it comes back to the Superwoman/Superman complex: You are in charge, you made a decision, you told Diane and the team and that was it. I think there's a better way, one that probably gives Diane the time she needs and avoids any potential problem with the other members of the team.

My solution is to get the team, or part of the team, together, explain Diane's situation and ask the team to come up with a solution.

I've taken the decision to the team, but note that I've only asked for a suggestion, not given them authority. There's a possibility that they'd make a terrible decision that I don't want to follow (it's my back door).

The team will likely say, "Let her go to the dentist and not worry about the two hours." They're likely to say this because that's how they'd like to be treated in a similar situation, and because it's the right thing to do. But they might say, "Make her take unpaid leave because she's pulling these kinds of stunts all the time." That might be new information for you!

But the real beauty is that, assuming you follow the team's suggestion, you now have buy-in. And buy-in is a powerful force. If you had made the same decision on your own it opens it up for some team members to bitch and moan about how you play favorites and give special treatment to anybody with a little kid. This way, you didn't make the decision, they did!

An added bonus: When you give the team buy-in, they feel that they have some control over their destiny. Rules aren't dumped on them from on high—they actually have some say in how the team, department, or company is run.

This approach might sound logical and easy, but it kind of goes against everything the buck-stops-here culture leads us to believe makes a great manager. Isn't it just a sign of weakness to outsource decision-making? We live in a culture that tells us only the weak avoid making a decision. In truth, a smart leader does make the decision but gives the team input.

Serve with sympathy

Don't try to pretend that everything's OK when it's not. Your team can smell it.

Let's say you're having a bad morning. Your car broke down, it's pissing down with rain, and you don't have an umbrella as you walk a mile to the office. Oh, and you've had a huge fight with your partner that morning and last night your dog died. When you arrive, do you smile and tell your team, "Morning all"?

Trust me, they will see through that. Tell them about the car, the rain, the umbrella, the fight, and the dog. And how will they respond? If you're in the UK, we all know what they'll say: "Can I get you a cup of tea?" Tea cures everything!

The real risk with an I-can-handle-anything attitude: credibility and trust. Once people catch you pretending, they'll never know when you're being honest. When your team doesn't trust you, you will not get the best from them.

Let's look at another sample situation. Let's say you're managing a phone team of 10 people. (Could be any kind of team.) And every month you measure every individual on a score of 0 to 10. One team member is Bill, who has struggled. You've worked with him and his score has gone from 3.0 two months ago to 3.5 last month. Then there's Fred, the team star. He's usually number one in the team, but if he's not then he's number two. Two months ago he scored 7.4 (best on the team) and last month he was 7.5, which again was best on the team.

You're going into the team meeting where you'll review the scores and you want to say something nice about Bill, who has really pulled his socks up and, if he can keep the momentum going, could be a good performer. What do you need to do first?

That's right: Stop at Fred's desk first, tell him you're going to say some nice words about Bill in the meeting because Bill has pulled his socks up and had a good month. Then tell Fred he's a truly valued star.

Communication, communication, communication. If you don't do something like this you risk angering Fred and hearing him mutter, "So, to get some praise around here you have to be really rubbish to start with?"

You don't want that. Let me ask you a question: Who's more important, Fred or Bill? What do you think?

When I present this scenario in training sessions, most people say they're of equal importance. And that's an admirable, egalitarian answer.

However, I say bollocks to that. Fred is definitely more important! He's 7.5! It doesn't mean you won't spend more time with Bill, but Fred is definitely on a higher rung of the importance ladder. Let me put it another way: Let's say your boss comes to you and says, "We've hit a rough patch and I have to sack most of your team. You can keep one person." Who do you keep? Would you even contemplate keeping Bill ahead of Fred? Well, there you go. Fred is really important! If Bill can boost his score to 7.6 on a regular basis then I'd go with Bill, but as it stands, Fred is your man.

The point is: Don't forget your stars. You need your stars. You can't hit those targets yourself but the more stars you have, the easier it gets.

Now, did you know that little Jonny loves to fish with his grandfather, Diane's dad? Maybe you didn't, but I hope his manager did. To be a great leader you have to understand what makes your people tick. I suggest that a manager sit with each person in his or her team and chat. I even recommend that you keep note cards or a file of some sort on each person. That way, at a glance you'll know who has children and their (approximate!)

ages, where folks like to go on holiday, what their hobbies are, and the rest.

The more you know them (the better your data), the more efficiently you can use the levers at your disposal to inspire them to ever-greater things. Let's say you want to have a team contest and you offer a bottle of champagne as a prize. Well, if you knew that half your team were teetotalers then I'd hope you'd realize that champagne is not the best motivator. If you knew that everyone on the team liked to go camping, offer a tent as a prize.

If you could get 20 percent extra effort from every person you manage, every day, can you imagine how powerful that would be? But you have to be a great manager to do that.

Remember: If you're doing your job well you're going to be very tired when you get home each evening. This is why. It's not the business decisions that wear you out, it's thinking about the people around you from the moment you get near the office until you're well off the premises. Every day.

Seriously, folks

✓ Remember that everyone is different. Welcome weirdness.
✓ Leaders come in all personality flavors.
✓ Write your own eulogy; it focuses the mind.
✓ Leaders are always being watched. Behave accordingly.
✓ When you get near the office, it's curtain up!
✓ Buy-in from staff is invaluable. Keep your stars happy.
✓ Your team members have lives—learn about them.

CHAPTER 12

IMAGINE THAT!

When I think of innovation and creativity, the numbers 12, 15, and 10 leap to mind.

No, they're not just the jersey numbers of some excellent quarterbacks in American football (namely Tom Brady, Bart Starr, and Fran Tarkenton, the most creative of all).

To me, those numbers are all about car insurance. That's right—they represent a bit of creative thinking that I'm especially proud of, because they led to a breakthrough in our business. I'll explain in a bit.

You'll recall that the third of my keys to becoming a great leader (after decision-making and people skills) is innovation and creativity. Great leaders keep thinking of new ways to do things, new ways to lead people, new ways to appeal to customers, new products to sell, and new ways to sell them.

If I asked you if you thought the world would be the same or different 10 years from now, you'd certainly say "different." But how will it be different? We don't know. Look back 10 or 20 years and you can see huge changes that were unforeseen back then.

The world changes because people are innately innovative and creative. In business you also must be innovative and creative or you'll be left behind. Staying the same in a changing world is not an option.

Creative people know that not everything works—and that reflects a flexibility that is crucial. They're eager to test their innovations and try again if they don't work. If fear of failure puts you off testing ideas, then you're unlikely to take creative risks. Innovation is part of Admiral's history, both internal and customer-facing.

Which brings me back to 12, 10, and 15.

In the UK in the mid-1990s, pre-internet, a 12-month car insurance policy was standard. If a customer called around to four insurers, she would receive four quotes. She'd choose one of the quotes and be all set for a full year, 12 months.

The next year the other three companies would send that customer a letter saying "We're better this year" or "We've lowered our prices this year" or whatever. The customer had gone from being an active shopper in Year 1 to being a passive shopper in Year 2. It was called a re-mail program, and we did it as well.

One day David and I were sitting around trying to think of a way we could get our customers out from other companies' re-mail programs. We wanted them to ignore the offers from other companies and stick with us.

We toyed with the idea of a 15-month policy. When they got the re-mail pitch, they'd think, "Oh, I'm good with Admiral for another three months," and toss out the mailing. But the 15-month idea had drawbacks. Charging a 15-month premium up front would make our sticker price a lot higher than the competition. Not attractive! And what if we took on a customer for 15 months and realized we hadn't done a good job underwriting him—we'd be stuck for those extra three months. And even then, he'd still receive re-mails from our competitors at the 12-month mark and might investigate, even if he was covered for another three months. So, no—a 15-month policy was not going to work.

Well, we thought, what if we went the other way? What if we offered a 10-month policy? Hmmm. Lower sticker price, less underwriting commitment, and our renewal notice goes out two months before the customer receives the re-mail from our competitors.

This was looking pretty good. But why would anyone buy it? What's in it for the customer?*

In the UK market there is something called No Claims Bonus (NCB). For every year a customer does not make a claim they get credit for a year's NCB, generally up to five years. In the UK, each company can do what it likes with its NCB tables and rates (unlike in other countries with similar systems where the regulator controls the pricing). We could offer a huge discount after one year, while other companies might offer a big discount for going from Year 3 to Year 4.

Also, a customer's NCB number was portable. If someone had four years' NCB with a competitor we would rate them on four years' NCB when they came to us. Our competitors would do the same.

Light-bulb moment: What if we moved customers up a year on the NCB schedule after just 10 months?

This was potentially very important to our customers, many

---

* Remember, it's all about the customer!

of whom were drivers with zero and one year's NCB. Throughout the industry the biggest jump in discount was from Year 0 to Year 1 and the second-biggest jump was from one to two years. We expected our customers would love this. They could go from zero to one two months faster and get all the way from zero to five years in 50 months instead of 60.

So we tested it. We did some trade-off analyses to see if consumers would choose a shorter policy even if it cost more on a monthly basis but less than the total sticker price of a 12-month policy. We found they would. Perhaps everyone thinks the future will be better and so they are happy to pay less today and pay again in 10 months, when they believe they'll have greater resources.

We needed to charge a bit more because the set-up costs had to be paid for over 10 months rather than 12. Strictly speaking, 10 divided by 12 equals 83.3 percent, but we charged around 86 percent of the 12-month premium for the 10-month policy. But consumers were so keen to move quickly up the bonus ladder they didn't mind this small uplift. Another beautiful twist: The competition could never catch up! Even if our customer called around when their policy came up for renewal at 10 months, the re-mail letter the competitor would send the following year would arrive 12 months later. The other insurers didn't know she'd taken a 10-month policy with us.

The upshot was that our customer always had to be an active shopper, never a passive shopper, and that meant they were more likely to stay with us. Nice.

Our idea clicked. In its heyday the 10-month policy accounted for half of Admiral's new business sales. And it accomplished a big goal: taking people off the cycle for other companies' re-mail campaigns. This meant the renewal rate was better among these customers than those on a 12-month policy.

IMAGINE THAT!

This episode demonstrates the value of throwing out the rules—at least at the brainstorming stage. So what if policies were always 12 months? There's no law. It's just another hidebound custom. Look at everything with naïve eyes; constantly ask, "Why?" like an eight-year-old: Why are they 12 months? Because that's the way we've always done it. Why? Because the year is a traditional unit. Why? Because the Earth revolves around the sun? I don't know why! You'll reach a point where customs seem ripe for change.

As a manager, it's up to you how to foster this spirit of creativity. Could be a suggestion box, virtual or real. Could be meetings with rapid-fire ideas, blurted out without fear of judgment. There is research that suggests a handful of people are best for productive brainstorming: too few and the creative sparks won't fly; too many and people tend to "hide" and not contribute.

In the case of our re-mail breakthrough, it was just David and me, sitting in an office with a couch and small table. We were discussing re-mail letters and the idea of tweaking the scheduling. The whole thing took maybe 90 minutes, and then we started doing some research.

No magic—except maybe isolating ourselves to avoid distraction. Creativity can spring up anywhere.

Another breakthrough, the creation of the Diamond and Bell brands, was classic innovation-by-theft—a time-tested business practice.

The first few years were very successful for Admiral. But there was also a huge growth in the number of direct-response firms. In January 1993 we were the seventh direct writer to enter the game. About three years later there were more than 20!

With so many new firms, there was much more advertising

than before, and getting noticed was getting harder. In the insurance industry there was a belief that you plough money into your brand and that's it. This was illustrated at the time by AXA, the giant French insurer, which was snapping up numerous companies in those days, including a few in the UK. The first thing they would do is change the company name to AXA. They threw away a lot of brand equity by doing this. But they believed that one brand around the globe was the way to go, and supporting more than one couldn't be efficient.

We took a counter-intuitive view.

Let me set the stage. Let's assume a simple world with two advertising pieces: Yellow Pages (YP) and TV. The YP, literally a thick book of yellow pages filled with company listings and adverts, was the Google of its day.

YP charged by the size of the insertion. At one time there were some 75 pages of car insurance adverts in YP books. All companies throughout the book paid the same price for the same-sized ad. So if you were advertising lawn care and there was less than a page of adverts you paid the same price as someone advertising car insurance, even though there was clearly great demand for space by car insurers. In short, YP was a very cheap way to advertise so we put in as many ads as possible for the Admiral brand. But to drive more volume we had to go on TV. Television was expensive, and generally the more you did, the higher the incremental cost.

It was David who hatched the idea to create another brand. That way, we could re-saturate the cheap source of business, the Yellow Pages, and reduce our dependency on the expensive source of business, TV.

This was heresy in the insurance world. So we loved it even more.

But it made sense if you looked at other industries (with larceny in your heart). When you go to the shampoo section at any large supermarket or drugstore, you find a slew of brands. They have shampoo for long hair, curly hair, bald people—everyone. And if you turn those bottles around, you'll find that many of them are manufactured by the same producer. Few manufacturers, many brands.

What seemed madness in the insurance industry was ho-hum-of-course in the Fast-Moving Consumer Goods (FMCG) world. By deploying a lot of brands, a single shampoo manufacturer got a lot more shelf space. If they just had one all-singing, all-dancing brand then they would get X amount of shelf space. But if they had five different brands, they'd get something near five times the shelf space.

The Yellow Pages was our shelf. By offering another brand or two we got a lot more insertions (shelf space) while reducing our dependency on pricey TV advertising. We just stole—er, borrowed—a page from someone else's book.

We created Diamond in 1997: a brand for women (men could be on the policy, but not as the main driver). We chose this target market because a) it was large, and b) women responded to targeted advertising. When we advertised "Cheaper Car Insurance for Women," we found that not only did we get a lot more response from ads in YP, we got responses from people who weren't responding to Admiral's plainer, vanilla "Cheaper Car Insurance" ads.

Stand out on the team: Dream up a scheme

Sometimes setting yourself apart just takes a little thinking and a bit of guts. In our course on Organizational Behavior at INSEAD, a two-hour, on-the-spot essay would determine our grade. The quirky professor (he claimed he owned a whale penis bone) said we should try to make our paper stand out—because he had 172 of them to read.

Challenge accepted. Now, I'd always liked rhyming books as a kid. What if I wrote my essay in rhyme? Nothing Shakespearean, mind you. More like Dr Seuss meets Org Behavior.

I practiced a bit and thought, "Why not?" I could try it for the first 30 minutes of the test and if it was working, just keep going. If I was struggling, I'd use the rest of the time to write a regular essay. (That was my backdoor escape.)

I sat down at the exam and read the case study we were to analyze. Well, I can't hide my pride—I hit my stride. I wrote eight pages, all in rhyme. It was great fun—and I thought my analysis of the case was quite good too! Then I held my breath.

We got our grades a few weeks later and, lo and behold, I had the top mark! The professor even invited me and two other students to his house for lunch—all down to my rhyming essay. (He really did have a whale penis bone! That's what he said it was, at least.) I met the professor again almost 30 years later and he said no one before or since had written their final exam in rhyme.

IMAGE THAT!

Lessons here? I think they're clear: Sometimes just think like a kid and you can be different; have fun and solutions may appear; combine a "difference" with quality and you've got a great chance of a breakthrough.

Diamond worked quite well, but at the same time we also introduced Bell for young drivers. We burned through about half a dozen different propositions for Bell over the years, including at one time being the insurer for people with zero NCB and then, soon after, being the insurer for people with five years' or more NCB! None of them had the same compelling proposition as Diamond had for women.

There was also a creativity knock-on effect from multi-branding. We were creative in how we organized ourselves in this new, more complicated, multi-brand world. It's my belief that you get more energy from small teams. So all three brands—Admiral, Diamond, and Bell—uniquely ran their own operations. There were shared resources, like finance, people services, IT, etc., but all the customer-facing areas were distinct per brand.

We continued this with the introduction of Elephant.co.uk a few years later. Eventually the advent of price comparison destroyed the efficiencies we had created by having independent brand operations. Wait—efficiencies? When each brand had its own customer-facing employees? I accept that one could look at this structure and see some redundancy. Each brand had its own CEO, for instance. You might be able to manage with only one.

Managing people at a distance is harder than managing people you see every day (or almost every day).

The biggest challenge of distance management is keeping in touch with the people who need you. In an office you can always find 10 seconds to say hello. From a distance, not only is it harder to communicate with people, but the people you manage need that communication more.

Most people who work from home work on their own. In an office, there is eye contact, conversation, all the distractions of an office—but now they are on their own. They need contact, they need communication, they need someone to show they care. More than ever they need to know that what they're doing is worthwhile.

To be a great manager who rarely or never sees his or her workforce face to face, you need to be creative. You need to be imaginative in how you communicate. You need to communicate all the time and then you need to make sure your communication is heard, watched, read, etc. So it can't be the same thing every day.

If you're sending out a regular video, one day it could be about the department, the next day you could show people how to make a pizza (I know a manager who did this and it's brilliant!), the third day it could be about your cat, and the fourth day it could be a serious management topic. Your people should look forward to getting the link to today's video.

Besides daily or very regular communication like an email, video, or audio report, managers need to call staff randomly, just to see how they're doing; they need to send handwritten thank-you cards so staff know that what they're doing matters.

I think a lot of managers started off in the Covid era with good intentions. But they never expected it to go on for so long. So their communications burned out. You need to make a plan. You need to map out your communications a month or two in advance. Of course things can change, but if you map it out ahead of time you'll see where it's getting dull or where you've sent 11 straight days of emails and need to do an audio tape.

Managers should also avoid falling into the trap of having only pre-arranged meetings. Sometimes you just need to pick up the phone and call someone without making an appointment first. In fact, I challenge you to make an unscheduled call to one manager every three days. I think you'll be amazed how pleased people are to hear from you.

But I think these are false economies when you consider the benefits of having someone senior dedicated to thinking only about that brand. Moreover, having separate organizations sparked inherent competition between the brands. Each operation would work hard to come up with new ideas to be better than the other brands. We were able to test new ways of doing things on smaller platforms and spread it over all the brands. In addition, we could benchmark internally.

It seems counter-intuitive that having separate operations could be more efficient than one big operation. But such is the power of having people directly involved in the business. That's easier to do when each person can see the value of what they do every day. The bigger an operation, the more difficult it is for people to believe their individual contribution matters.

This belief generates extra energy, which outweighs the added cost of having more managers. It's one of the reasons small start-ups often outperform large, experienced companies with deep pockets.

The success of small organizations is a great management lesson for us all. The more you can make each individual feel like their contribution is important, the better chance you have of getting maximum effort from them. And that's just easier to do if the team is small.

Remember Excite? How about Ask Jeeves? Lycos? Alta Vista?

They were all search engines that launched before Google. And they're all in the rubble that created the pavement for today's giants. We had a similar situation with Elephant.co.uk.

In the late 1990s, along comes the internet and everyone is trying to figure out how to make the most of this new thing. The company that built the first online quote-and-buy engine in the UK, Iron Trades, spent a fortune building it, which crippled its short future.

In those dial-up days it was probably doomed to fail.

But Iron Trades set the standard and gave the rest of the industry something to work with, test, and improve on. They paved the road and the rest of us just drove behind. I'm a big supporter of this strategy. Beats trying to break new ground all the time. That's hard work!

Our internet strategy, and that of our competitors, was to be everywhere. Most firms offered their services on the internet and over the phone. Let the customers decide. There was Direct Line with a phone number and DirectLine.com. We had Admiral.co.uk and Admiral on the phone.

But we saw an opening for a pure internet play. There were already pure internet companies like Amazon and easyJet. The perception among consumers was that anything internet was going to be cheaper. (Very often it was!)

We launched Elephant.co.uk on August 2, 2000. You really had to work just to find a phone number. There was no phone number in the advertising and you had to dig through several pages of the site to find one. Yes, we did take sales calls and we did all the after-sales service over the phone, but most of the sales process was done on the net.

Every kick is a boost

Many years ago we lived in a cul-de-sac that had five other houses. One evening I arrived home at the same time as a neighbor and went over to say hello. I could see in an instant that something was wrong. His posture was poor and his face very pale. "I don't know what I'm going to do," he told me. "They made me redundant. I'm 50 years old and out of work."

He had been working for a major utility company for 25 years and was convinced that he'd never be able to get another job and take care of his family. He had four children between ages eight and 20.

But he received a good redundancy package that gave him time to think out his next move. He realized he had valuable knowledge that could help the then-new mobile phone companies get power to their phone masts.

The result: He built a multi-million-pound business over the next 15 years, finally selling it and making millions himself! But he never would have built this business and made those millions if he hadn't been forced to do so. Necessity was truly the mother of his invention.

THE THREE KEYS TO SUCCESS

One pleasant surprise was that consumers would often do the entire quote on the net and then call us to purchase. Back in 2000 people didn't feel as comfortable parting with hundreds of pounds without talking to someone. For us, it meant the calls were much shorter than usual, so our salespeople were far more efficient. The customer (and computer) did much of the work!

And to think we almost pulled the plug. Elephant got off to a slow start as we struggled to get our message across. We weren't far from shutting it down and shifting investment back to the Admiral brand, either by internet or phone. But we stuck with it and did a TV ad in February 2001, and Elephant took off.

That ad highlighted the message that "if it's the internet it must be cheaper," which clearly resonated with consumers. From that point on, Elephant was a freight train. That lasted until the development of our next innovation: price comparison. We launched Elephant with zero customers in August 2000, and when the Group went public on the London Stock Exchange in September 2004, it was our biggest brand, having caught and passed first Bell, then Diamond, and finally the Admiral brand itself. In four years!

A little tangent: Nothing succeeds like success. When Elephant got moving in 2001, every day seemed to be better than the day before. The atmosphere in Elephant was amazing. Staff came into the office every day almost giddy. When a manager said, "Good morning!" she meant it. And team members scarcely needed encouragement. Nothing succeeds like success.

Do you see the common threads in these stories? These innovations didn't happen because we were insanely creative folks. Flexible and open-minded, sure, but not Dalí-like creative.

Practical is more like it: Each idea tried to solve a problem. It turns out necessity really is the mother of invention. But you can still help the mother along. Here's how:

Approach an idea by pushing your thought process to the extremes. What if we gave it away free? What if we charged £50,000 for each one? What if we were open 24 hours? What if we were only open for business hours and closed at lunchtime on Fridays? Push hard at either end and you improve your chances of finding the right place somewhere near the middle. This is where open-mindedness and flexibility—and, sure, creativity—come to the fore. If you don't push to the extremes you won't know what you're missing.

Art and commerce

Just pushing your ideas to the extreme isn't enough. You need to get your entire team thinking that way as well. If the team seems caught up by reality, try taking them to an art museum or get a coffee table book of Dalí's works or Picasso's or Van Gogh's. What were these guys smokin'? Whatever it was, maybe you and your team need some. Metaphorically, of course.

Distracting the team with art is one way, perhaps music another. Kids' books can be great, too. (My favorite is *The Boy Who Ate Flowers*, by Nancy Sherman—all in rhyme!) Hopefully the imagination that created these stories can rub off on you and your team. And then you need to get them to reapply this imagination to their world.

But pushing to the extremes takes confidence. You are probably going to come up with some pretty stupid ideas at the extremes—I know I have. And if you can't stand someone saying, "Well, that's a pretty stupid idea," ideally while laughing, then you're in trouble. If you don't find that a laughable idea, then you probably aren't pushing hard enough. Managers ask me how to stimulate creative thinking with a team that's been together for a long time.

First, there are great benefits to a stable team: People know each other, know how to deal with each other, trust each other, and aren't afraid to speak their minds.

The downside is that they can begin to accept answers and solutions without adequate challenge. How do you get fresh thinking from this group? You have to work at it, you have to stimulate it.

You're a manager—manage!

I've found that exposing them to art, music, or a new environment can trigger fresh thinking. The key is to get your team out of its rut. Shake people up by showing them that there are different ways to look at the world.

Stimulating creative thought can be hard work. Like everything else in management, there is no magic recipe. But being creative really helps when it comes to trying to get others to be creative.

If you've read this far, I guess I'm a pretty good leader—you've followed me deep into the book. If people follow, you're a leader, remember? Let me recap the keys to being a good leader. It all starts with making good decisions by gathering data and listening to other opinions.

This is followed by people skills, like lending support, granting autonomy, being approachable and making people feel valued for their contribution; get the most from everyone around you.

And, lastly, creativity! Don't be afraid to be different.

All of these are general themes to think about and weave into your management style. What follows are some practical tools you can use right away.

IMAGINE THAT!

Creative sparks

✓ The world is changing. You should, too.

✓ Push ideas to the max—and beyond.

✓ Steal from the best.

✓ Let someone else do the paving.

✓ Small groups foster competition and let individuals shine.

✓ Success is really fun.

✓ A melting clock can speed up innovation.

PART 4
THE PRACTICAL

CHAPTER 13

BALANCING PRIORITIES

Remember the chapter where I told the founding team of Admiral that I promised to work long hours—but that I'd also have breakfast and dinner with my family? I managed to keep that pledge, for the most part.

But with those time-dependent bookends, how could I—or you, or anyone—get everything done? You probably have more things to do than you have time for. And it's a constant battle to ensure you are doing the "right" things. I don't have a magic formula for priority setting, but that won't stop me from sharing some advice.

Probably the best advice I've ever been given came from a boss early in my career after I asked about setting priorities. "What's the goal?" he asked. Whenever you're struggling to decide the order of tasks, he explained, ask that question, followed by "What's the shortest way to get to the goal?" Such simple yet such valuable guidance. If you don't get to the things on the bottom of your list, they shouldn't matter—or they should matter much less than the things you actually get done.

Here's a related principle I learned early on that is important for a busy manager in a busy office: Do not be the cork in the bottle. Don't let things sit on your desk with people waiting for a response.

We're all busy. You're a busy manager, your staff are busy on projects, proposals, tests, you name it. But just because you're busy, you shouldn't make your team wait. If you find that you are slowing others down, then review how you're spending your time. Few things are more demoralizing for a team than to work hard on something only for it to sit on their manager's desk for days—or weeks!—without being looked at. (I can see you all nodding in agreement. Don't be that manager.)

But how does this advice help you when you simply have more things to do than you have time for? Ask yourself: What would happen if I didn't get X done? If your answer is that the business would grind to a halt, I suggest you should get X done! Here's a tip to keep your office humming: If leaving something on your to-do list unfinished will screw up someone else's list, move it up your list and finish it.

Now I'd like to demonstrate a magic trick. Chances are your list got so long because you thought you were the only one who could do certain tasks. You didn't delegate. So here's the trick: You delegate more, your list gets shorter, and things get done more quickly. Bonus: The team is happier. Get other people to make the decisions.

I know, this is easier said than done, as we discussed previously. Very often, as managers and leaders, we're convinced only we should do some jobs, and we think it's a sign of weakness to delegate.

Wrong. Delegation is key to growing your team, your organization, and yourself. If you cannot delegate, then what you're managing cannot get bigger than you. This is the third time I've addressed this—that's how important it is. Remember my father's meat company? It employed about 30 people at its peak. He could not grow his business further because he could not delegate. He had to be involved in virtually every decision. Thus, the business was restricted to what one individual could do.

> Once you've set your priorities, question them. That's right—a good manager is constantly questioning his or her priorities. The world moves fast and if you don't review priorities often, you are likely to do things that aren't all that important. Take a moment and look at your to-do list and ask yourself: Is this really important?

I know that nervous feeling when you don't take part in everything. When I was a young CEO and Admiral was growing, I would worry about some of the decisions those around me were making. But I fought the urge to get involved. Grrrr! It was hard to do! But now I'm very glad I did.

I knew that my butting in would either limit our growth—or prevent me from getting home for dinner.

And from this acid-churning moment of letting someone else make a decision came the true beauty of delegating: watching others step up. I was always a big believer in giving others a chance; this gave me even more faith. I believe everyone has good in them until proven otherwise. I became convinced that everyone is capable of doing great things and you should let them go until they reach their limit.

Sometimes I think the word "manager" in business becomes abstract—it's a title, a box on an org chart. Instead, think of it like the manager of a sports team. This person manages players, people with goals of their own, and it's up to that manager to help individuals improve so the team can work as a unit. Same with you. In team sports it's the team that wins trophies.

My goal as a manager is to get the best from everyone I manage. It's not only best for the company, it's self-serving as well. I know that if I can get the best out of the people I manage then I stand a far greater chance of blowing my targets out of the water. If I do that then I'm seen as a great manager. The more I believe in the people I delegate to, the more likely they are to surprise us both and tackle those challenges, often far better than I would

Beware the Logo Police

They amaze me, the stupid, low-priority things leaders often get involved in. Always ask if you're using your scarce resources—time and energy—wisely. Also, don't ask others to do stupid things.

Example: logos. Many organizations have precise rules about logos and typefaces for presentations. When I was with Churchill, we were owned by a large Swiss company that was very pedantic about the use of its logo. It had to be a particular Pantone color and set in the lower right-hand corner on a page—never at the top! If you didn't comply, the Logo Police came calling. This is so wrong.

I agree that consistency is valuable, but the customer is not sitting at his breakfast table, saying, "Wow, honey, look at this! The logo on this letter from Admiral is slightly lighter than it was on our certificate of insurance!"

Nobody cares! You've got far more important things to deal with. Same with PowerPoint fonts: Molly uses one typeface and Billy-Bob uses another. Before you make someone spend an hour synchronizing typefaces, ask yourself: Does this really matter?

It doesn't.

have done! Yet another benefit: They then have more confidence for the next challenge.

One more note about priorities and food. You may have noticed I've stressed the importance of meals—those breakfasts and dinners at home. Don't worry, I haven't forgotten lunch. Here's my advice: Always take it.

Always take lunch. This is a bedrock principle.

It's not about the food, it's about getting out and clearing your head. Lunch at your desk or in a meeting is fine once in a while, but after four or five hours of work in the morning, you need a break. (If you don't—hmm, how hard were you working?) If you want to have a productive afternoon, get away from your desk and clear those cobwebs. You can take a newspaper, magazine, your phone, a friend from outside the company, or, sometimes, an office colleague. But give yourself a fighting chance for a tip-top afternoon. There will be occasions when you won't be able to get away, but that just makes getting away every time you can even more important. Put lunch in your diary. Block out an hour for yourself.

This is not just about your afternoon productivity. It's about maintaining a high-intensity work rate month after month, year after year. This is a cumulative phenomenon, like an exercise regimen. If you skip lunch or frequently have it at your desk, over the long run you will burn out. Who wants a burnt-out you?

You might even start to resent the company—which I resent! The company never told you to take lunch at your desk every day.

While we're at it, let's go well beyond lunch: Take your holidays. I always urged my team to do so.

The power of motherhood

In 1993, near the end of our first year of trading, two senior managers, both women, came into my office, closed the door, and sat quietly. They hesitated, then told me that they were both expecting.

I've since learned that such closed-door moments usually mean a baby is on the way. And now I think it's wonderful.

But in 1993, when those key managers told me they would soon be going off for several months, I thought the sky was falling. Over time I have come full circle. I now think maternity is brilliant, and it benefits everyone. Here's what it means:

- **She's committed to the company.** When a woman makes this announcement, she's several months pregnant and it'd be very difficult for her to switch employers. For at least five months she will definitely stay with the firm. Can you really say that about anyone else in your office?
- **She will return energized.** It's my experience that a woman returning from maternity leave is amazingly efficient and organized. She has to be! Making sure her job and family are looked after takes impressive dedication.
- **It's a chance to develop your bench.** When you promote someone to fill in for the person on maternity leave, you'll find out if that individual is up for a greater role. Make sure the fill-in knows it's temporary, so if it doesn't work out it's not an

awkward demotion. If it does work out, move them back but tell them that they've impressed and could be in line for the next opening.

- **Mothers are brilliant managers.** Raising children is a great school of management. Her perspective, her priorities, her communication skills all are sharpened. A woman returning after having a child is a far better manager than before.

As time went on, when a woman would come into my office, shut the door, and sit down quietly, I would think, "This is great! She gets a baby and the company gets all these benefits!"

Now paternity leave is also a reality. I must admit, I don't have experience with that but I can't believe it would be much different for men spending time with their babies than women.

Coming from America, where 10 days is the typical amount of holiday people received, maybe 15 days if you'd been in the job a while, I was aghast when I saw in the UK that new starters would get 20 days' holiday! (In Italy it was 30. Yikes!) Turned out this madness had a method. (Maybe time to move to Italy?)

I learned that this is better for the company in the long run. Having four weeks' holiday allows people to go off and recharge their batteries several times a year. I wanted to see my managers take a week every quarter and possibly two weeks straight once a year.

I would frown upon those who were "too busy" to take holiday during the year and then have to take two or three weeks in December. I was a big fan of "use 'em or lose 'em"—if you didn't take your 20 days in the calendar year they disappeared like smoke. You couldn't carry them over to the next year. That wasn't unfair: It reminded everyone to take regular holidays, not work for two years and then take a month off.

This isn't just about productivity. Managers who don't take their holidays are likely to be blinkered by their business. Managers need to get out, see the world, have new experiences, break away from routine, and get a fresh perspective on life and business.

When you're on holiday, don't hesitate to talk with people, find out what business they're in or what job they do. Ask how their business or office is organized, how they got started, what their challenges are. (Oh, and buy them a beer.) It's stimulating to think: "What would I do in their situation?" And it might give you a different way of looking at your own challenges. (Heck, buy them another beer and then tell your stories; they might have suggestions.)

Managing and leading are stressful. Most businesses, even good ones, are packed with problems, deadlines, and difficult decisions. You've felt that pressure. I always thought I reacted pretty well to stress; I got used to it. It didn't seem to faze me after a while.

But less than a year after I semi-retired people were already telling me I looked five years younger. Most of you don't have the luxury to semi-retire and de-stress, so do the next best thing: Take regular holidays!

Priority list

- When setting priorities, ask, "What's the goal?"
- Find the shortest route there.
- Don't cork up anybody's bottle.
- Delegating works like magic.
- Go out for lunch.
- Get home in time for dinner.
- Take your holidays.

CHAPTER 14

GET OFF YOUR BUTT!

Your people need you. Many of them are chained to their desks by phones or computers, but you, as a manager, have freedom of movement. So get out there! Make small talk. Make big talk. Be seen. Ask questions. Listen to what people have to say.

It's incredible how much you can learn about your business, your customers, and the competition, just by getting out of your chair and walking around. Don't be the manager who wonders what people are saying. Be the one who knows what they're saying.

In this day and age, it's easy to stay busy sitting in front of our screens—answering emails, checking results, finding information—and feel like you're accomplishing something. Which you are, to a limited extent.

But it takes effort to get up and walk around. Somehow it doesn't feel as productive to walk around and talk with people, compared to shrinking your inbox. But I'd argue it is even more productive. It's just that this productivity manifests itself differently and does not always provide the instant gratification we have come to crave.

Speaking of cravings (back to food again!), my wife and I are not all that fond of Chinese food—in the abstract, anyway. But, strangely, almost every time we eat it, we love it. So it has become shorthand for us: When we face something that we don't really want to do but may end up enjoying, we turn to each other and say, "Chinese food."

We learned that when we dive in, we'll be glad we did. That's how it is for getting out of the warmth and safety of your chair and walking around to hear what people have to say. Engage with them, show interest, make a comment on what they're doing— and most of all, listen to what's happening on the ground. It's Chinese food. You'll be glad you did.

Sometimes when talking with team managers, I'll propose this scenario: You're managing a team in a call center and wallboards are going nuts, flashing 100 calls waiting. What do you do?

A practical prank

One time we felt our sales managers were spending too much time at their desks and not enough time out and about. We came in one morning, gathered all their chairs together and tied them up in the middle of the room. The managers couldn't sit down all day. A great way to get them to go walkabout!

The right answer is to go to the manager of the team next to yours and ask her or him to cover your team for an hour. Then you jump on the phones and start taking calls.

Come on, Henry—is that really the right thing to do? Big deal, the wallboard now flashes 99 instead of 100. So what? Why jump on the phones when the problem can't be solved by one person?

Here's why: leadership. If you've read this entire manual you know the answer. Your team needs leadership; your people need to know that what they're doing is important—so important that the manager is pitching in.

I've heard excuses why a manager won't jump on the phones. "What if an agent has a question but now there's no manager to answer it?" Or, "What happens to that important report my boss asked me to write?"

On the first excuse—that's why you ask a nearby manager to cover for you today (and tomorrow you'll cover for her or him). Yes, that manager will be stretched, but that's OK for an hour. And consider this: If you're not there, maybe the agent will be forced to think a bit harder and answer the queries him or herself. They may learn that they can take initiative. You're delegating! What's really the downside risk? That one or two customers will need a callback later? Is that really so bad?

What's important is that your people don't become demoralized by that flashing callboard. There's a negative correlation between a demoralized team and call center efficiency. And I'd wager this goes for equivalent situations in every department in any company.

When they see you jump in with them, you earn their respect. And every time you give out a "Let's give great service!" message, they know you mean it. They see that when the going gets tough, you're shoulder-to-shoulder with them, giving that great service. The more they know that what they're doing is important the more likely they are to take it seriously and do the job well.

Here's a bonus benefit to jumping in to help: You'll understand and appreciate their work. It's an eye-opener! You'll experience exactly what we're asking the agents to do and the pressure they're under. Trust me, you will step away from 60 minutes on the phones with a to-do list as long as your arm.

And that report your boss wanted? The one that'll be delayed because you helped out? Tell your boss you were busy making customers happy. That should buy you extra time.

One more thing about jumping on the phones. You're someone with a fair amount of ego. I know this because you've climbed to a management position, and you need some ego to reach a senior position in any organization. But you have to check your ego at the door when you come into the office. Nobody is too big to pitch in.

I'm not saying you should be egoless. (Nobody would accuse me of being egoless!) But you have to manage your ego, rather than the other way around. This dovetails nicely with the keys to leadership we've covered—communication, trust, reward, fun, creativity, and the rest. In all of this, I hope you've sensed my overarching message:

It's not about you. It's about them!

You can't hit your targets yourself. So, help the people who will help you hit those targets.

To do that, you need to suppress your ego. If your ego gets the best of you, you won't get the best from your people.

I have seen many bright, talented people fail to become great managers because they were more concerned about making themselves heroes than hitting the team's goals. They thought they could do everything better than everyone else. They cared more about their own well-being than that of the company.

Blow your targets out of the water and you can be great. You are not great by showing how smart you are in a meeting and then strutting out, displaying your peacock feathers.

Walk the walk

- Get out of your chair.
- Talk. Ask. Comment. Listen.
- Pitch in—you'll earn respect and learn a lot.
- Check your ego. It's not about you, it's about them.
- Chinese food is great!

The more you focus on you, the less chance of success—for you or your team. And beware of the flatterers around you who will pander to your ego and make you feel like the center of the universe. This may feel good but doesn't help you get the job done.

I know I told you to switch your mindset to "curtain up—everyone's watching you" as you approach the office. But remember to resist hubris. And that's hard to do. You have realized you're on show every day, but that the show isn't really about you. Keep things in perspective: You are only great because the people around you are doing great things.

Make it your morning mantra. When you walk into the office, mumble quietly: "It's not about me, it's about them."

Basic training

Even bosses need training. In fact, every boss, manager, or leader should go through their company's entry-level training, then actually do the entry-level job for a week.

Few companies do this. It took me about 15 years before I did this and I can only ask myself why I didn't do it years earlier. I learned so-o-o-o-o much!

I learned about how we train people. I did my training with a group of senior managers, so it was a bit different to joining a group of new employees. We did it this way because we needed to do the training twice as fast as the usual three weeks.

As a group we were stunned by what our people were being taught. Some things were just plain wrong, some were not quite right, and some made their future lives more difficult.

But we got through the training, even taking the practical exam all new salespeople have to take (and pass) before they are allowed on the phones. Then we spent the next few days on the phones taking calls from customers. Here we learned how really difficult these jobs are. Trying to co-ordinate working the system while making conversation with the customer, while moving quickly so as not to waste time, while remembering all the regulatory rules we needed to follow, while trying to build rapport, while trying to make a sale... well, you can see, it's a lot! We gained a huge amount of respect for the people who do the job every day and take call after call after call day in, day out, week in, week out, month in, month out from customers.

We also had the pleasure of finding out first-hand what's really important to customers. That was great knowledge to have. It's amazing how patient a prospective customer can be if you just communicate with them, tell them what you're doing, and why.

For instance, we had to be prepared to answer calls from people who had completed the form online and were now calling through to ask a question or to purchase. With these people we had to do a data protection check so we'd know we were talking to the right person. Amazing how much easier this was if you just said, "I have to ask you some data protection questions now, this is for your protection," versus just asking the questions. Same is true after someone made a purchase and we had to deliver a rather wordy regulatory spiel. We were obliged to give them this information, even if they didn't want it. But if you explained that the regulator thought this was for their benefit rather than just launching into the talk, they were much more receptive and patient.

In the grand arc of your career, two or three weeks of getting your hands dirty with the business is fantastic experience for you. Great to understand what your people are being asked to do. Great to learn what customers are all about. And, extra bonus, you also get a lot of street cred with your team.

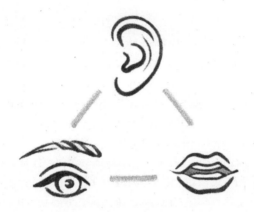

CHAPTER 15

LISTENING AND SPEAKING

When you decide to implement an idea, who is the ultimate judge of your decision? Is it your immediate supervisor? Is it your team members? How high can we take this exercise—maybe the CEO?

You're looking in the wrong direction. It's not anyone who might be looking over your shoulder. It's the people outside the office.

It's the customer. It's the marketplace.

And yet it amazes me how many decisions are made, or ideas implemented, without consulting that ultimate judge. Of course, it's easier to turn to Billy-Bob at the desk next to yours, or Betsy at the next meeting. That's not enough.

We all have customers. Communicate with them. Find a way— pick up the phone, open up an email, get some carrier pigeons, whatever, but do something to discover what these very, very key people in our business think. Do it regularly and get those around you to do it as well. Just call people and say you want to ask them a couple of questions. And then try to find out what they do and why they do it.

Well, you might say, don't we have people who do this? Marketing departments spend huge sums on focus groups and customer research. And these days we are peppered with feedback questionnaires after virtually every transaction.

No doubt, this is important. But for the cost of a few minutes you can do your own research and it can be every bit as informative as a high-priced official report. I feel so strongly about this that many years ago we launched an initiative: Every manager would talk to a customer every month. Just one. And then we'd get together at the end of the month and each manager would talk about their call.

Fascinating stuff. We learned that people didn't always behave as we expected. In fact, "didn't always" could easily be "hardly ever"! We learned that customers often picked up on a single thing—maybe a phrase in an advert, a box on the home page, or one line on the phone—and based decisions on that. We learned that customers are busy, and don't spend the time and effort to think through all the messages we're sending them. (But wait, what could be more important in their lives than car insurance?)

When you're talking with a customer, you need to probe. You need to keep asking questions about what they did and why, what they didn't do and why. For example, if you're talking to a customer about a recent service experience, ask how they went about it. Website first? App? Phone? If they went to the website, what happened there? Did they consider webchat? If they didn't, why not? Do they use websites or apps for other services? Do they ever use webchat with other companies? What types of companies are those? The more you ask, the more you learn.

If that sounds like a lot of time in your busy schedule, it's not. If you do a single call each working week, that's fewer than 50 calls a year. Not a lot. But I promise you, you will learn something about your business from every call. By communicating regularly with customers you can be much more efficient in choosing the projects that need to be worked on because you will know where the value lies.

One time, in one of the non-UK markets, I found out something shocking that should have had huge ramifications on what we sell. We asked customers about the price of some ancillary products. What we learned was that anything under $10 a month (not annually!) was considered "incidental." Holy cow! All we need to do is find two or three good products that we can retail for less than $120 a year (not exactly the lowest bar in the limbo game) and a lot of people will buy them. They told us $10 a month is just a couple of coffees or two beers a month. Knowing a little bit about how customers think can lead to big differences in the bottom line.

Staying close to your business means staying close to the people who pay the bills: your customers. Again, this isn't altruism, though of course it's always nice to be of service to strangers! No, it's about the bottom line: If you know more about your customers' behavior than your competitors know, that translates into a true competitive advantage.

The customer, the customer, the customer

It was Christmas Eve many years ago and my wife's family was staying with us. We thought maybe we would give a little extra something for the guys in the family. So I went to Boots in Cardiff, which is a big store, much more than just a pharmacy. It was, as you can imagine, very crowded.

I found a good gift item, which was a package of four travel-size colognes. I grabbed five packages (big family!) and queued up to pay.

After at least 10 minutes, it was finally my turn. I put my five items in front of the lady behind the till and reached for my wallet. "Did you know", she asked, "that these are three for the price of two?"

Clearly I didn't know this, otherwise I would not have taken five. I looked behind me at the ever-growing queue and realized that if I went to get the sixth one, which would be free, I would have to wait in line all over again. I was ready to say, "Just charge me for these and don't worry about it," when the lady asked, "Which one do you prefer?" (There were three different sets.) I pointed at one of the packages.

She got up out of her chair and made her way into the store. I lost sight of her but waited where I was.

After a few minutes she came back to her position behind the till. She had the package of colognes I'd indicated. She rang up my entire purchase, this last package being free.

Wow! That's service! This lady did not have to tell me that there was a three-for-two special at all. She didn't have to fetch it herself. She took the initiative to get up out of her chair and go and get me the item, which she then gave to me for nothing. Stunning.

And here I am, decades later, still singing the praises of this lady and Boots.

How do you bottle this attitude and spray your entire workforce with it? How do you get every member of your team to think customer, customer, customer, regardless of what position they have in the organization or what they do?

THE PRACTICAL

In the early days of Admiral, I used to help train our sales-people. One exercise we did was to break into small groups, just four or five of us, and go into stores in Cardiff to see how the service was.

I learned that if I was a bank robber in 1993 I'd know exactly where to hide: a jewelry store in the middle of the city. Because once you stepped inside you became invisible! We could get nobody to help us. I once walked around for several minutes without attracting any attention before approaching a salesperson sorting rings behind the counter and asked if she worked there.

Without exception, every store we went into, jewelry or other-wise, the service was terrible. The employees didn't care, didn't know their products, didn't ask how they could serve me, etc. All it would take would be a bit of training, attention, and motivation and I am certain these stores would have sold a lot more product.

Remember CDs? When they were new, I took a little group into a store to buy a CD player. When we finally got someone to show us how the machine worked, he couldn't get it to play! He assured us that when it did play it sounded really good. How did he expect me to buy one when he, the supposed expert, couldn't make it work?! All he had to do was get to work five minutes early and make sure he knew how they functioned. But, clearly, he was neither trained nor motivated to do this. So we walked out of the store without buying anything. At some point the store owner is probably going to think it's all about price and start offering discounts to make sales. If only the store owner took the time and trouble to train and motivate their people they could make a lot more sales without having to cut prices and margins. Peo-ple go into stores for a reason: to buy things! If they walk out of the store without buying something then somebody hasn't done their job right.

LISTENING AND SPEAKING

As a manager you have a responsibility to train your people and make sure they are motivated to give great service to all customers, internal or external, all day, every day. There are times I've stayed in luxury hotels and come away shaking my head at how good the service was, in large part because *everyone* gave me good service. It was not hit or miss, it was hit and hit! The service chain is only as strong as the weakest link.

Good service starts with simple things: Don't make people wait, treat everyone with respect, answer questions accurately, do what you say you're going to do and keep communicating. I don't care what industry you're in, whether you're in the public sector or the private sector, whether you do manual labor or analyze data, everyone has a role to play in giving good customer service.

Every organization has customers and without those customers there is no organization. Therefore, it's pretty simple: You'd better pay close attention to those customers!

Rinse and repeat

There's the evil *1984*-style brainwashing, and then there's my kind. Brainwashing is a manager's secret tool of communication. If you keep repeating the same messages or actions, people will come to think they're the norm.

If you have an egg-timer meeting every morning and end it with "Let's make every customer happy today!" and do this day in, day out, then people start to think that making customers happy is the norm. Nice.

Unfortunately, I've also seen bully managers use this tool. The staff came to think it was normal to get a tongue-lashing from the leader if they did something below expectation. They were brainwashed to think that this was acceptable behavior. They figured everything must be their fault.

Brainwashing is a powerful tool. Understand it and use it wisely.

THE PRACTICAL

Managers need to understand their customers and what's required to give those customers service that falls somewhere between acceptable and incredible. That means the manager has to be close to the business and close to the people on the front line.

Many, many years ago we had a situation where we messed someone about with a claim. Hands up, we were guilty. So we offered the customer £75 as an apology for the poor service. The customer was happy with this and asked if we could just take the check to her bank and deposit it for her. In the UK you could deposit checks like this and most major banks were likely to have a branch nearby.

What did our staff member say to this request? Gulp. Our staff member said, "No. No, I can't do that." Ouch.

Some of you might fault the staff member and, certainly, the staff member could have done better. But I fault the manager. If asked, the member of staff would have said they couldn't leave their desk and the office for 20 minutes to go into town and deposit the check. It isn't known if the manager truly would have been upset to find the member of staff away for 20 minutes, but that's not the point. Perhaps the staff member would have gotten a dressing down or maybe she would have gotten a bonus. We don't know. The point is that the member of staff thought the result would be negative. The manager had not imprinted the idea of doing whatever it takes to help a customer.

If you are going to manage people to give good service then you have to make sure they know they have the tools to provide that service. If our staff member was leaving the office twice a day for 40 minutes each time to deposit checks, then maybe the manager would have to call that person to account.

What happens in most places is that rules appear. One person does something that isn't efficient and everyone gets a new rule: No depositing checks for customers. Rules are bad. Rules stop people from thinking. They stop people from doing that little bit extra. If Boots had a rule that said, "No one behind the register can go away from their till," then that lady never would have been able to give me such great service.

Throw away your rules and let your people do things. You'll be surprised how good they are. And, if they're not, then you need to train them better. And if that doesn't work, then you need to replace them.

As important as it is to learn how to listen to your customers, as a manager it's just as important to learn how to communicate with your colleagues. Your ears and mouth are important, sure, but the key is your eyes.

Here's a trick that works in a one-to-one meeting or even a small group of three or four. Make it a habit that after you leave a meeting, you can remember the color of the eyes of the others who were in the room. (OK, all you clever folks: If you're in a country where most people have the same color eyes, be prepared to describe their eyebrows.)

If you can't tell the thickness of someone's eyebrows, then it's likely you haven't been looking them in the eyebrows. And if you haven't been looking them in the eyebrows (or eyes), then you probably aren't connecting with them. And if you aren't connecting with them, how can you expect them to trust you, believe in what you're saying—and follow you?

A meeting is for meeting. With people. Not for scanning the markets, reading emails, or checking your diary. All of these hinder your communication. If you're one of those who checks your phone during a one-to-one meeting, you are not respecting the person sitting in front of you. And for goodness' sake, don't make your golf dates!

That one-on-one rapport is important and rewarding. Another approach is the good, old-fashioned personal note. Don't underestimate its power, whether it's a quick email or handwritten. Save those for key moments for maximum impact.

Then there are emails to your entire group. Good moments for these notes: announcements about profits and losses; big events in your own life, like a marriage, birth, graduation, a great holiday. Share yourself with your team and wind in a few good business messages for motivation.

Business is a marathon, not a sprint. You need to find moments to help recharge your team's batteries.

My favorite time to do this was New Year's Eve, in an email to the senior managers. It's the ideal moment to recap the year, to look forward to the next year, and to include a bit of a personal message as well. The "fresh start" at the new year is particularly true in business because you generally have a new budget and new targets. As I said in one letter: "Right now everyone is on budget! Yay!"

Here's an example—my New Year's Eve letter from 2014:

Hello, New Year's Eve.

Well, we're mopping up another year; turning another page; opening a new diary (or perhaps a new app!). It's an odd moment, moving from one year to the next because it's both a time for reflection and anticipation.

On a personal level I had a very good 2014. Four of my many 2014 highlights: shaking hands with Warren Buffett, playing golf with Ian Woosnam, winning my FINRA case against those bastards from ***** (power to the people!) and *power walking with Diane at dawn in Seville, Rome, and Paris. How about you? What were your highlights?*

On a professional level there were many highlights. Here's the short-list: looking at the numbers on the wall in the renewals department of Admiral Seguros, a bigger number for every month! Seeing ConTe profitable (WOOOOOOOOO!!!!!); Rastreator's doubling of profits; Martin telling me I can have a Brian toy for free! Compare. com getting paid by Google; the Spanish IT team delivering a US system to the French business on schedule; the Loi Hamon—may I live long enough to see it enacted; the new agreement with Hannover Re for Elephant; seeing so many staff in our new offices near Delhi; performance of the back years in UK motor; sales numbers from home insurance; the incredible move from Cap Tower to our own custom-built home, Ty Admiral… the list goes on and on.

I feel there's a lot of positive momentum in the Group at the moment. If it wasn't for the 2014 loss ratio in UK motor, I think we'd be in uncharted positive momentum territory. Of course, today the UK motor loss ratio is, undoubtedly, the single-most influential number on Group performance and right now 2014 is pretty ugly. So we shouldn't lose sight of this while basking in the sea of success just about everywhere else. And I know those in the UK with a power to influence this result are working flat out to do so.

Beyond UK motor all the businesses have done a lot of growing up over the last few years. Today I think all these businesses are highly focused on realistic targets. That sounds a simple sentence but it's taken us a long time to get there. I think we've got very good teams of people in place and I can see that much of the foundation digging we've done over the last few years is paying off. I spent a lot more time, particularly in the second half of the year, visiting the non-UK operations. These were generally longer visits, which were much less rushed and allowed me to get a much better feel for each organization and the people in them. Here's the amazing thing: Every time I left one of our offices I left with more energy than I'd come in with. I was constantly surprised and inspired by how much all the people in each organization care about their work and their company.

And here's what the future comes down to: Can our people do a better job than the competitors? Trust me, it isn't about whizzy technology, it's not about magic algorithms, nor is it down to award-winning adverts; rather, it's down to the people who give you whizzy technology, magic algorithms, and winning adverts. And please never forget those people who just answer the phone or an email nicely and make a customer smile. All our people are very important—duh, that's why we hire them. But the people I'm writing to now have the greatest influence. We are the ones the others look up to: for instruction, for motivation, for direction, for energy, for hope, for clarity, for purpose, for care. This is the group of people that wields the power and carries the responsibility. My advice? Treat the power with respect, for power is an inherently unstable element and so can be dangerous. And feel empowered, not burdened, by the responsibility: This is your chance—grab it with both hands and make the most of it.

I feel that only time will prove my next words true: This is an exceptional group of people that can and will do exceptional things. I have, at one point or another, worked with everyone receiving this email and I believe that each of you is very strong individually. But the path to success only begins with bringing talented individuals under the same corporate roof. If Admiral Group is going to reach its full potential then we must follow the path that unites us, takes us on a journey where the sum of the parts is greater than the individual pieces; that is, we are far, far better as a team than we are as individuals. I know for a fact that I am better because of you. You have all played a positive part in my growth and development, you have helped me to do my job better and I hope each of you can look around and say the same thing about your peers.

I am very proud of what we're doing throughout the Group.

I am proud of our spirit of innovation; our ability to do analysis without paralysis. I'm proud of the way we stay close to our businesses and our people (no offices in Admiral Group and only one hedge). Last, but not least, I am proud of the way we run our businesses, the way we treat our customers, our staff, and each other. I consider myself very fortunate to be a member of this team.

I am really keen that 2015 will be a great year for Admiral Group. I will certainly give all my effort to make it so.

I wish each of you and your families a successful, prosperous, healthy, and happy 2015.

Happy New Year – Henry

As effective as the written word can be, nothing beats in-person communication. I was talking recently with a senior manager about improving his ability to inspire and motivate his team. So I did my Tom Cruise impression. No, not really—but I did tell them to think of how a *Top Gun* pilot locks on to a target, when that circle on the radar screen doesn't let go. Likewise, lock in on people's eyes when talking with them. Hold those eyes until you get some reaction to what you're saying. You can do this even on a video call! Don't be distracted when you do this. I know, if you're standing in the office it's easy to let your eyes drift to what's going on over the shoulder of the person you're speaking with. Don't do it! Hold those eyes.

Interestingly, this also works with large groups. I groan inwardly when I see someone get up in front of a group and before they've even settled into a position, they've started talking. Whoa!

Here's how to address a group: Get in front of your audience and say nothing. Look them over and lock eyes with a few people (can't do them all, I know!). Only then do you start speaking. You'll be amazed at how many more people will be listening.

And during your talk don't gaze over the heads of your audience. Look directly at people. Lock eyes where possible.

Then there's the finish. One time I watched an excellent team address by a senior manager in ConTe, Admiral's Italian insurance company. He delivered a great talk but while he was finishing it, he started to walk off, trailing off with a few thank-yous and blah-blah-blahs. Painful to watch such a good talk end in such a limp fashion, with his last two sentences being said while on the move, facing away from his audience.

You want your talk to have impact, to leave an impression. And that means you need to work hardest on the close. The thing that the audience most likely will remember is the last thing you tell them.

So use the same technique as you did at the start. Pause, lock eyes for a second with one person, then another, and pause again.

You're opening a space for your closing line and you've got the audience leaning forward, anticipating…

Only then do you give them those closing lines. And when you're done speaking, stop. Don't move. Stand there and count to yourself to three. Then move. You've got this!

Talking points

- You might have never met your real boss—the customer.
- You should get to know her.
- First-hand intel is the most useful.
- Look into—and lock on to—colleagues' eyes.
- Speak to groups as individuals.
- Use dramatic pauses to get their attention.
- Nail the dismount!

Curtain's up!

Playing a Lost Boy helped me find my voice when I grew up to be a businessman.

My school district was able to fund a professional theater company called Theater 65 (the number of the district). Cast and crew were recruited from the junior high school, and the high school, and some of the actors came from nearby Northwestern University.

Being a sports-loving kid, I wanted no part of this. But my mother, who loved theater, insisted I try out for *Peter Pan*. So, grudgingly, I did. And, much to my surprise, I got a part! I was Tootles, one of the Lost Boys. And it was fantastic fun—a whole new world opened up. I went on to perform in many more shows and learned to do crew as well.

I now realize how amazing and professional these performances were. They even rigged up a device for Peter and Wendy to fly around on! It was great fun and I became totally hooked (ha ha). We rehearsed each show for a couple of months, almost every afternoon after school, and then did around 10 performances over two or three weeks, with paying audiences of our peers and their parents alike. The pinnacle of my career was having the lead role of the Golux in James Thurber's *The 13 Clocks*.

I learned so much from these performances, including how to project my voice, how to command attention, how to use the variation in my voice for emphasis, how important timing is to audience comprehension, even things like how to stand properly and walk downstairs without looking (answer: Don't worry, the step will be there!). The post-show cast parties were a pretty good perk too!

Unfortunately, during my years with Theater 65 the school district ran out of money for programs like this. I can't remember how many car washes we organized on Saturday afternoons, raising a few hundred dollars every time (not bad for 1973!). But the car washes, bake sales, and all the adult fundraising wasn't enough to pay the brilliant people who ran Theater 65 and, eventually, it folded.

The lessons that helped my business career included being able to talk to an audience and knowing the co-ordination and attention to detail needed to make a presentation of quality. In particular, I learned to keep in mind that every time you speak to people—be they staff, peers, bosses, or third parties—it's curtain up, you're on. Finally, there was the key lesson that it took a lot of people to put on a great show—actors, directors, set designers, script writers, lighting specialists, even someone to pull the curtain up and down. In short, there are no small parts, only small actors.

CHAPTER 16

BUILDING YOUR TEAM

People—that's what all of this is about. Have you noticed? The recent chapters were about the people around you: how to communicate with them, treat them respectfully, reward them, have fun with them, lead them, encourage them, inspire them—you get it.

But where do these people come from? If they are the ones that you're going to need to blow away your targets, well, they'd better be pretty good to begin with, right?

Nothing is more important than selecting these people—the colleagues who will take this company into the future.

Confession: It's almost a coin flip that you get the right person in just the right spot. It doesn't matter what searches, psychometric tests, number of interviews, lunches and dinners, graphology reviews, or background checks you do, it's still kind of 50–50.

But I've learned plenty over the decades. After all, we started with five people scratching out a business plan in that dismal office, remember? Somehow we got from that handful to 10,000 employees of a highly successful multi-national corporation that is consistently named one of the best companies in the world to work for.

My biggest lesson in building a staff: Recruit talented people, install them at a level lower than you think they should ultimately be at, give yourself time to learn what they're really like and really good at (and not good at!), and then move the right ones into positions of power and influence.

When it comes to doing it the other way—hiring straight into senior positions—my experience is poor to middling.

This means a different way of recruiting. Many leaders and managers recruit to fill vacancies. This is where I have the poor experience. But if you continually recruit good people and build a surplus of talent, when those vacancies appear you can fill them with known quantities. This is a *huge* lesson: Fill vacancies with known talent.

But it's still a challenge to find and recruit those talented people! I've found it helps to act like a selective university. Early on, I repurposed a selection of questions from the Graduate Management Admission Test (GMAT)—the standardized entry test taken by hopeful business students (like me in 1987).

Knowing your colleagues well is crucial to a well-run company. To help our managers bond, we borrowed an idea from the *Sunday Times*. The newspaper's "A Life in the Day" feature is an account of a typical day of someone in the news, but with tangents that provide insights into character and motivation. It's a fun, revealing column.

So I asked each manager to write one, to open up about themselves. Just a page or two about a typical day—but I encouraged them to take detours. For example, "I always have toast for breakfast" is mildly interesting, but the detour—"Growing up, Mom used to give us big, beautiful pieces of toast for special occasions"—makes it intriguing.

We compiled the stories in a book, complete with photos of the writers, and each contributor got a copy. It was fantastic. The stories were universally humorous and revealing.

We did it three times over 12 years, with a changing roster of contributors, though quite a few were in all three editions. It was interesting to compare their lives across time.

Not only was it fun to read but it gave the company snapshot memories of the people who ran it in those moments that cannot be recreated. It also enlightened the senior managers about their peers. This was especially valuable as we expanded internationally because many of the managers were not based in the UK.

We printed up extra copies and used them for recruiting. If we liked a candidate, we'd give them a copy and told them that these would be the people they'd be working with. It was a warm, human touch and candidates loved it.

This is what I mean by creative management. We took an existing idea and used it for a totally different purpose, in a management context.

The GMAT is academia's way of taking people with different degrees from different universities, different work experiences, backgrounds, and so on, and finding a way to compare them. My selection (from a practice exam) is one complete set of verbal questions and then most of a quantitative (math) section.

Before giving anyone else the test I did it myself and eliminated the really hard math questions (perhaps you remember my struggles with advanced math). I ended up with 25 math questions and 30 verbal questions. I entered everyone's scores, verbal and quantitative, in a spreadsheet. As my data sample grew, I had a better tool to measure someone's score against.

I did the scoring this way: I added up all the correct answers and subtracted all the incorrect answers. I felt this was important; I didn't want people guessing. If they didn't have a clue of the answer, I wanted them to leave it blank. This way I could tell risk-takers from conservatives. Risk-takers guessed, conservatives left questions blank. But here's something interesting: In all my years of giving the test no one asked me how I scored it. If someone had, I would have skipped the test and hired them on the spot!

Unlike the real GMAT, my test had no time limit. But that doesn't mean time wasn't a factor. I could learn a lot about a candidate by checking how long it took them to finish, coupled with how many questions they answered and how many they left blank. If someone took a long time and left many questions blank, that told me that they were risk averse. Perfect for some jobs, not great for others. Someone who does it quickly and answers all the questions—while missing some—is a risk-taker. You can only gain this information if you don't limit their time.

That spreadsheet was just the start. As years passed, we saw a strong correlation between the people who scored well—but not excessively well—and great managers. The maximum score was 55 (25 + 30). The sweet spot for managers who would have people management responsibilities was somewhere between 25 and 45. There can be exceptions, of course, but people who scored outside that range, at either end, were typically less successful on My Three Things that Make a *Great* Manager. The math score was a good proxy for analytical skills. Remember, I had removed all the really hard math questions, allowing only questions I could do! When someone had a low math score, we'd suspect they might not be able to interrogate data and make good decisions based on data. For some jobs, that was fine; for some jobs, the people skills, the verbal skills, were more important. But for jobs where you wanted an analytical mind you really wanted a high quant score.

This sounds very straightforward and reliable, and it was. But we still made mistakes—in one case, by ignoring test data staring us in the face. We paid the price later on.

This was for a very senior position, and strike one was not promoting talent from within. Our goal was to find someone more on the analytical side, although they would also have substantial people management and leadership responsibilities.

Strike two was letting time pressure catch up with us. We liked one guy in particular who scored 32 on the GMAT. Not bad. But within that 32 it was something like 8 on the math and 24 on the verbal. Just the opposite of what we were looking for! Strike three!

We hired him anyway and—surprise, surprise—it turned out badly. In particular, he did not seem to understand the ramifications of spending lots of money on advertising that didn't bring a return! He was very poor with data, so he didn't bother with it. (Any strikes left?)

As for those verbal skills, they were certainly polished, but it was just a veneer. The first time people met him they almost

Think differently?

People sometimes tell me they recruited someone they didn't really get on with in hopes that this person would bring a different line of thought to the table. Makes me cringe.

My view is that each of us is quite different. We are all diverse, if you will, and if you can add to that by hiring people of different ages, genders, and so on, that's great. But don't think you're getting diversity by hiring people who don't think like you. All you're getting is trouble!

Why? Because they don't think like you! You don't need everyone to have the same exact thoughts (it'll never happen) but you do need people who are happy to share in the way you are trying to do things.

And you need to nurture an atmosphere where people are unafraid to speak their mind. I'd wager you get more fresh ideas and intelligent pushback from a group of people who like each other and share a similar outlook on life than you would from a group of people who "think differently" from each other.

universally thought he was brilliant. The second time he was OK. By the third meeting everyone began to wonder.

So, three mistakes: 1) hiring someone who we didn't know to go straight into a senior role; 2) being pressed by time; and 3) ignoring our own data, which was sending a clear message that this was not the profile of the person we wanted.

Everyone has their own interviewing style. Let me share mine with you. I'm not saying my style is perfect or that no other style will work. But I've tested mine over hundreds of interviews and it works for me.

I'd start the interview by holding up the candidate's CV and saying, 'Here's what I know about you. There must be more. Put some meat on the bones.'

And then I'd sit back and see what happened.

I rarely stepped in to say anything while they were going through the CV.

Some people started with their youth and 35 minutes later they had not inhaled.

And they were only up to their university days! They did not get hired. Some people, particularly MBAs, were able to deliver their CVs in 80 seconds. This other extreme was not quite right either. There must be more to you than 80 seconds!

Some of the things people told me when putting meat on the bones were crazy. I learned the insides of companies I never knew existed and cared nothing about. I had one guy say to me, "I really shouldn't be telling you this but…" and he proceeded to tell me some worthless office gossip concerning a politician. He was right—he never should have told me!

The worst response when I asked them to put meat on the bones was, sadly, one of the most common.

"Where should I start?" they'd say, and I would groan inside. That showed me that they were unprepared for this interview.

Let me ask you: If you were making a presentation to the board of directors, would you ask the board where you should start? No! You'd start by highlighting the key aspects of what you think is important.

Well, isn't a job interview one of the more important things you do in a career? You might think that when asked to talk about their CV, an obvious prompt, people would know exactly what to highlight before digging into the pertinent aspects of their history. Amazing how that never happened!

So I was already judging a candidate by how they started, what they chose to highlight, how much worthless information they talked about (a lot!), and how long they took to go through their history. All of these acted like a giant interview question with the added bonus that I also got an insight into their history.

Once they'd gone through their CV I was done with their history. Some good recruiters dig deeply into the candidate's experience. That's not my style. My reason: A candidate can fudge answers about their past to make them seem terrific in any circumstance. My time is limited, so I liked to give them situation questions to see how they think—especially questions where there really isn't a right or wrong answer. Often I could see them trying to figure out what answer I wanted to hear. These no-wrong-answer questions told me a great deal about what the candidate would be like to work with.

I like to start with a fun, easy question that tells me a lot about the candidate's confidence level and ambition. "It's 10 years in the future," I say, "and I'm walking through an airport and stop at a magazine store—should there possibly be magazines in 10 years' time. I see *Fortune* magazine and, lo and behold, it's your picture on the cover! Why? Why are you on the cover of *Fortune* magazine in 10 years' time? What's the headline and what's the story?"

I get very interesting answers. Some people have great social purpose ("Lifting poverty in Asia", "Helping women to better education levels"), others talk about running their own business, or a subsidiary within a company that has created something new or had a stunning success. I like to see if they talk about being on the cover because of themselves or because of being part of, or leading, a successful team. Once I was flummoxed by this answer: "I don't think I could ever do anything to get on the cover of *Fortune!*"

Next I like to ask questions that force the candidate to think on both sides of a question. I'll give them a situation and ask them two reasons why they should do X and two reasons why they should do the opposite. It's important that senior people are able to think on both sides of a problem and not just fall in love with their point of view.

Here's an example. For about 20 years we had a small business within Admiral Group called Gladiator Commercial, a broker for small-van insurance—the electrician's van, the plumber's van, the florist's van, things like that. Gladiator had a panel of insurers from which it offered rates, unlike getting an offer for car insurance directly from just Admiral. Gladiator then got a commission from the insurer for each sale. Gladiator was a solid, self-contained business, profiting between £2 million and £3 million a year. At its peak it employed some 170 people, in an office separate from the rest of Admiral. It had its own computer system and small IT department. It was a very consistent performer and required next to zero capital, as it was not the insurer. My interview question: "Give me two good reasons to keep Gladiator Commercial in the Group and two good reasons to sell it."

In the "keep it" option I was watching for over-thinking. I'd hear candidates give two very sophisticated reasons for keeping it—and often ignoring the fact that it made £2 million to £3 million every year. Hey, what's so wrong with that? With no capital injections? But that was too obvious for many candidates.

On the "sell it" side I was waiting to hear those two familiar and ridiculous words: "not core." Maybe it was personal: That's what we were told back in the late 1990s when our parent company was looking to get rid of us. Sure enough, some candidates would say we should divest ourselves of Gladiator because it was not core, even though it was self-contained and made a tidy return every year.

Now if a candidate explained that "not core" meant we could redeploy the resources used by Gladiator for greater gain in the "core" business, then fine. But just to say "not core": sorry, not good enough.

Most candidates gave reasonable answers on both sides of the question. I still marvel at one who gave me the two reasons to sell Gladiator, and when I asked for the two reasons to keep it, they simply said, "Well, I think we should sell it." And that was it. Perhaps a good answer, but not what I asked for.

I also had questions where I listened to see if people were just trying to please me with the answer they thought I wanted to hear, or if they looked at it in practical terms and gave an answer that made business sense.

One of my favorites:

You're the CEO of a company based in Cardiff, Wales (surprise!). You have a big call center operation. Not long ago you opened up a call center in Halifax, Canada because the time change allows you to staff there in the afternoons to answer UK calls in the UK evening.

The operation is going very well and growing rapidly, as is your core business. You send people from Cardiff out there regularly to stay for a week to six months and help with management, human resources, training, and the like. As both a cost measure and as part of the culture of

The Cleveland airport test

When my senior people were recruiting, I'd ask: "Does the candidate pass the Cleveland airport test?" No offence intended to the good people of Cleveland, but if you were delayed for four hours in the Cleveland airport with Candidate X, would you be wishing for a quick, painless death, or would you be happy to spend that time with them?

If it's the former, then you should think twice or three times before hiring that person. You need to get on with the people you manage.

And don't let technical brilliance trump the airport test. A genius who comes across as awkward or belligerent is no bargain. Hiring someone you don't want to spend time with, or just don't like, even if they are a genius in their field, is a recipe for disaster.

the company, everyone who flies to and from Canada flies economy class.

One day you're sitting with your feet up on your desk (as you
do) and your finance director (FD) comes into your office. He
says, "Boss, I've got to go to Halifax next week to sort out the
new office space because if we don't get more space and hire
more people we'll have to slow down our growth rate and that
would be silly. I'm going to go on Monday morning, I have a slew
of meetings lined up, including the local press and the Chamber
of Commerce, plus meetings with staff and sorting out the lease
for the new space. But don't worry, I'll take the late flight back
to Heathrow on Tuesday night, land Wednesday morning, have
a car bring me to Cardiff and I'll be on time for our big meeting
with the ABC corporation on Wednesday afternoon. By the way,
I'm planning to fly business class."

OK, job candidate: What do you tell your FD?

Many candidates think I want to hear how the culture is sac-
rosanct and that the FD cannot fly business class. Some mention
the cost. So that's most often the response: The CEO tells the FD
he cannot fly business class.

That's sort of OK to start. We then do a little role-play where
I'm the FD pleading my case. "But, Boss, how will I be of any help
with the ABC company on Wednesday if I haven't had any sleep?"
Most candidates will hold their ground—no business class. The
better ones try to find different days to do the trip (not possible,
we need the new lease ASAP) or ask if a subordinate can be sent
(nope, no one understands these things like I do). And then, as the
FD, I'll ask, "OK, what if I upgrade myself?"

Sometimes, despite all the talk about how important the culture is, the candidate will cave in and say, "Yes, that's OK then."

That's really the wrong answer because it misses the point. No one who might see the FD at the front of the plane is going to know who paid for it!

It sorts out the cost issue, but it doesn't do anything for the culture issue. We continue in this vein until I'm sure the candidate is not going to do any further thinking about it and that his or her mind is made up.

Here's what I was looking for: someone thinking it through with rational business sense. I wasn't looking for someone to stand on the culture soapbox and make decisions for the business that are counterproductive. In this case, the FD needs to fly business class, otherwise his or her work, both in Canada and back in the UK, may suffer. Culture is important, but culture is there to help the business, not damage it. I'm looking for someone who can work within the situation to make a rational decision.

A rational thinker would remember that in the story I told them the people who went to Halifax stayed a week to six months. It would be no problem for these people to take a day's rest to get up to speed. If you're only going for 48 hours your rest will have to come on the plane. The ideal candidate would say she'd create a new rule that would fit this and similar future situations—say, anyone going for 72 hours or less can, if they think it necessary, fly business class. This would apply to anyone, not just the FD. It's no longer an "us versus them" problem. You change the parameters from hierarchy to length of stay. You do not need to sacrifice the company culture to achieve a rational solution to the problem.

One key point about recruitment is time. Which is key to so many business decisions! We made our worst recruitment decisions when we felt under pressure to fill a particular position; when we didn't have time to keep looking. This is also why I like to bring talented people somewhere into the organization and then, when I know a lot more about them (and vice versa!), they can move up into bigger roles. When that particular position opens up, ideally you have several people in your ranks already who can step up, rather than have to fish desperately outside the company.

One last recruiting tip. After the candidate has left the office, talk with all the people who met the candidate, not just your close associates. People like personal assistants or folks from People Services who might have shown the candidate from interview to interview. Get their opinion. If the candidate was warm and smiley to all those he or she interviewed with but treated the "common" staff with disdain, avoid them. You know you'll be getting someone who can easily switch from one face to another. You want to hire people who treat everyone in the same respectful, friendly manner.

Recruiting board

- Hiring is crucial—now and in future.
- Slow down. This is important.
- Use a test to compare candidates.
- Don't hire people you don't like.

- How a candidate answers is as revealing as the answer.
- Regurgitating company philosophy doesn't trump business sense.
- Ask around before committing.

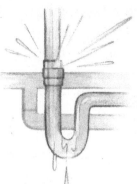

CHAPTER 17

IMPROVING AND REMOVING

What is the first thing you should do when someone makes a mistake? It's not a trick question and not a complicated answer: Figure out how to fix the problem!

The first thing you do when you have a leak is stop the bleeding. Apologies for the mixed metaphor, but the impulse works in all settings. After the damage is repaired you can go back and figure out how it occurred and assign blame if required.

But even then, before you lash out at the "guilty" party, ask yourself what your part in this problem was. Did you give the culpable people the right leadership? Guidance? Training? Time? Resources? In short, did you do everything you could to ensure that the problem would not occur? Did you have the right person in the job in the first place? Perhaps you should have done a better job selecting that person or teaching them.

And before you go rubbing people's faces in the problem, remember that this is a team. The team succeeds or fails together. If it's one person's fault, it's everyone's fault. Including the person at the head of the team—someone you know very well, someone with the ultimate responsibility.

Of course, you must discuss the problem and try to find the root cause. It is very important to know how mistakes occurred. But remembering that it's a team should affect how you go about making things better for the future. You might need to make changes that will be difficult for some team members to accept.

But I start from the point of view that no one is trying to make mistakes. That means you need to make your changes in a civilized, professional manner, not as part of some ego-fueled rant, as some managers do.

When I hear speakers say they "embrace failure," I say bullshit. I've never met a manager who wants failure in their organization and you'd be silly to be the first.

Sure, they're usually talking about how a failure taught them something or led to something good—but "embrace" it? That rings false. When something goes wrong, fix it. Think first about sorting things out, second about whodunnit, and third about how happy you are now that you've had a failure.

Look, we're all going to make mistakes. Some will be mistakes of judgment, some will be mistakes of carelessness, some will be mistakes of limited natural ability, some will be mistakes of communication, and there are certainly other types of mistakes lurking out there. Whoever never makes mistakes should toss the first stone. Mistakes, even failures, are part of life and part of business. The great manager helps people who make a mistake to learn from it and be better because of it.

The greatest failure is the failure to learn from failure.

Say a problem arises that means you're not going to hit your targets. You're tempted to let rip at someone. Take a deep breath. This is the moment you need to pick them up, not kick them further down. In my experience, the person making the mistake is probably feeling far worse than you are. Maybe they are even expecting a good kicking.

Instead, pick them up, dust them off, help them stop the bleeding and motivate them for a better day tomorrow. This is your moment to help someone improve. This is the moment they are most open to listening and changing.

Remember, you're dealing with people's lives. If you kick them, yell at them, or publicly humiliate them they have to live with that. They have to go home after work carrying that load you've dumped on them. Is your ego so big that you can't realize that you have no right to ruin their life outside work?

Of course, the nature of your reaction will depend on what's gone wrong. We had a situation once in one of our non-UK businesses in which a lawsuit had the long-shot potential to cost us a couple of hundred million pounds. It was a complicated story involving a third-party company, but we were the ones ultimately liable (because we didn't do a good enough job on the contract with the third party).

One of our most senior managers was running this business; call him Mr X. I got all the top senior people together and told them that this was not the time to kick Mr X even though the potential liability threatened us all. Instead I told them that this was the moment we had to pick Mr X up. It's not like he wanted the problem.

But this was the type of thing that could happen to any of us and therefore we all needed to help Mr X.

In private, I told Mr X the same thing and added that he needed to inspect his house to make sure there were no other problems lurking—showing that this was an odd set of circumstances.

If it's a one-off problem, that's one thing. But if the person persists in making mistakes, or this was the latest in a series of mistakes, well then, it's pretty simple: You've got the wrong person for the job.

Mistakes are one thing. But perhaps a more common personnel problem is motivating someone who doesn't want to be motivated. I was recently asked about this and was caught flat-footed. We've all encountered the problem child who doesn't respond to the normal stimuli.

For example, let's say you have someone, Billy-Bob, who does a good job—not record-setting but nothing wrong. There are other people who do less well in your team. But let's also say you think B-B has a lot of potential and you think he could really do good things in the future. How do you unlock that talent when it's not clear it wants to be unlocked?

What I do is give myself a time limit. That's right—I would give the time limit to me, not to Billy-Bob. The time limit is to prevent me from spending too much time on the problem. At some point I need to wave the white flag of surrender and either let B-B go or just accept that I will never get more than I'm getting now.

The point here is that you can't always solve all problems. Sometimes the best course of action is to realize that this one has gotten the better of you and you should just push on. No one wins always. A lot of managers have so much hubris that they cannot fathom not being able to "win." They fight battles that are just time-wasters long after they could have been productive elsewhere.

But before you give up, you should try! Start by trying to understand B-B. Talk with him. Talk with his peers. Talk with people who have worked with him in the past (perhaps even getting permission to speak with people who have worked with him in other companies). Find out what he likes to do when he's not working; find out what he does with passion (maybe it's painting or stealing cars, whatever). Be creative—the normal solutions don't work!

There will be times, however, when it just doesn't work. If you can live with a member of the team being less engaged than the others, fine, live with it. Otherwise, I see two solutions. First, move him somewhere else. Perhaps a change of scenery will motivate him. Maybe his passions and personality align better with a different position (or a different manager). You're a manager, remember? Maybe that middling midfielder would be a fantastic full-back.

The second solution is to part company with him. More on that in a bit. Don't think you're Superperson. Sometimes giving up is the right way forward.

Somewhere between transferring someone to another department and sacking them is the demotion. I've been asked how I do that. Answer: carefully.

This happens a lot, especially in young, growing organizations. You start the business with a small team. You're the CEO. You have six people reporting to you. But time goes on, the business grows and develops, and some of those six people excel but some don't. Meanwhile, to move the business forward, you hire additional senior people, perhaps to augment current roles, perhaps for new positions. Now you've got 10 people reporting to you.

The day arrives when you realize that you have to realign the org chart. You've got too many people reporting to you, or some of the people reporting to you should naturally be reporting to others, or both.

Training session

One leadership lesson has stayed with me since I was a teenager. One day my parents brought home a puppy. Prince was a great dog, but he didn't always obey us.

In those days "choke collars" were common—the type that tightened around the dog's throat when you pulled on it. My mother came home from a dog training session with Prince and showed us the right way to manage him.

She said the dog trainer explained that yanking on the collar made a dog want to pull the other way. The correct way was to gently pull on the leash and slowly tighten the collar. As it slowly tightened, the dog would follow you or react to your command.

This turned out to be a great management lesson, minus the collar. Telling someone what to do, especially senior people, is akin to yanking the collar. Their reaction is going to be to pull the other way. So you have to go slowly, build a case, get their agreement to the facts, introduce your ideas, and, as you go along, ask them if they understand what you mean. It's the equivalent of the slow pull on the collar. They'll follow.

You will have to tell some people that they will no longer report to the Head Honcho and that they are now going to report to one of their peers. Double whammy!

This is where you take great care. These are senior people, some of whom might have been with you a long time. They probably worked long and hard to get the company where it is now. And as a thank-you they are going to be dropped down the org chart!

I would recommend two things. First, a one-to-one with the person being moved down. You need to explain that this isn't about them, it's about you. You need to explain that you have too many people reporting to you, that your job is evolving, and that you don't want to be the cork in the bottle because you have too many reports.

IMPROVING AND REMOVING

You also tell them that with too many reports you will not be able to give them all enough time. Then you simply say that as a result of this the org chart has to change and here's how it's going to look going forward. As if it was the most normal thing in the world.

There will be a short time of choppy waters. But eventually those waters will settle down and a new normal will be established. Just get on with your job. Accept choppy waters. People will get used to it.

My second recommendation is to tell them that this is a great moment to prepare everyone for the future. When you announce all the changes to your senior team, tell them that you will be reviewing your reports and the org chart every six (or 12) months and that you expect more changes in the future. You're building in change as normal, something to be expected. For anyone who was moved, this eases hard feelings—it's part of the normal system—and may motivate them to move up next time around.

It's the same for meetings. For years you have the same senior team attending the same weekly meeting. But you need to shake these things up from time to time. You need to invite some new people and sometimes that means uninviting some long-time attendees.

My way to do it? End the first meeting altogether. It's finished. And start a new meeting with slightly different people. Give the new meeting a new name. Yes, you must explain the new set-up to the disinvited but that's easier to do when it's a new meeting with a slightly different footprint to the old meeting. Again, tell all who will listen that you will review all meeting groups every few months, which prepares them for future changes.

You never forget the first time. Certainly I'll never forget the first person I sacked. When I was managing the marketing and sales office back in Chicago early in my career, we had a young lady, let's call her Leslie, who was the office secretary. She opened the post, took care of the account-opening documents, answered the main phone, and picked up spillover calls from the sales department. She was a very nice lady and, in the beginning, did a fine job. But as time went on her performance declined. It got to the point where I had no choice but to let her go. This was my first firing and I was really nervous. I mean, Leslie had a family and I was removing her pay check from the family income.

I sat with her and we talked it through. I showed her the decline in her performance. What I found was someone who didn't really care. Not because she was an uncaring person but because she'd lost her enthusiasm for the job. I wished her well and told her I hoped she could find something she really wanted to do and, I said, if she did, I'd bet that she'd probably be quite good at it because she wasn't without talent. Leslie seemed to chew on this. She was not at all bitter or twisted. In fact, she might have been relieved.

I breathed a sigh of relief when that day was over. About 10 months later she came back to the office for a visit. She walked up to me and said, "Thank you." I looked about—was she talking to me? I wondered what the joke might be. She continued, "Thank you for firing me and suggesting that I try to find something I like. I took some time off to think things through and came to the conclusion that what I really wanted to do was teach. So, I got my teaching certificate and now I'm teaching. I absolutely love it. Thank you."

The thing with sacking someone is that they usually know things are bad before you've even decided to do it. They may not know they're about to be sacked but they're probably unhappy in their job. If people who like what they do, do it better, then people who are unhappy with what they do definitely don't!

That was my great lesson about firing people: If it's reached that point, they are probably pretty unhappy themselves. After my experience with Leslie I would start any firing by saying, "Well, you're probably not happy here, and to be honest, that shows up in your work, which we're not completely happy with." As often as not, you'll see them start to nod their head in understanding. Like I said, they know.

It's really a different way to look at firings. They aren't the end for someone but the chance for someone to make a new beginning, possibly doing something they really want to do. Sounds a little Pollyannaish but it's usually true.

Firing people is not always so clear-cut. There are times when you just have the wrong person in the wrong job. I remember once, many years ago, I was working in Paris as part of my time in the futures industry. I had a visit from an American guy who was working for the Chicago Mercantile Exchange in London. We had met before and he was a very nice guy. We were having (an excellent!) lunch in Paris and our conversation drifted off business to personal topics. He mentioned that he was divorced. Being curious, I asked, "What happened?" He paused for a moment and then he said something that lives with me to this day. He said, "She's a nice person. I'd like to think I'm a nice person. Together it didn't work." What a great way to sum it up!

I find that this logic rings true when parting company with a decent employee who isn't quite achieving what you want. It's also a bit of a nicer approach than telling someone in great detail what a worthless piece of garbage they are.

The hardest thing I've seen a manager do was when a senior manager of one of our non-UK businesses had to be sacked. It fell to the CEO, a woman who started that business from scratch. The manager was a very nice guy who would bleed Admiral blue if you jabbed a vein. He loved working for the business he was in and he loved working for Admiral Group.

If you spoke with him for a couple of minutes about what he

was doing you'd come away thinking here was a pretty smart guy. But if you spent 10 minutes with him you'd come away thinking, "Huh?" Everything he talked about became very complex, to the point where you had no idea what he was talking about.

This was at the height of the financial crisis and unemployment was very high. The guy was married with children. Ooof. But the CEO knew that she needed someone better in that role if she was going to meet her targets. Management doesn't get much harder than that.

She had about 250 people in her organization at the time. I wanted to make this difficult task easier for the CEO so I told her the following: If she doesn't fire this guy, she is being very, very good to one person but very bad to 249. And you really shouldn't penalize 249 people for the sake of one. That's very important for all managers to remember. As managers, we try to give everyone a chance, even a second chance, and maybe, just maybe, even a third chance. But at some point you have to think of all the others in the organization.

If anything, I probably worked too hard to save people. Interestingly, when we finally cut ties, the reaction from others in the organization is: What took you so long?

Corrective actions

- Problems need fixing, not yelling.
- You always carry some responsibility.
- We all make mistakes.
- Pick people up, don't knock them down.
- A person getting fired knows it's coming.
- Don't fret—they'll be happier elsewhere.
- But first, try giving them a different job.

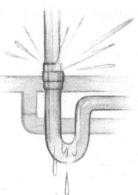

CHAPTER 18

MEASURE EVERYTHING

Those two words—measure everything—could be the entire chapter. Measurement is the key to knowing what's going on, what's changing, and understanding good from bad. To do any measurement you need data. But data by itself is not worth a lot. It's kind of like having the tires of a Ferrari but no Ferrari. Let me give you an example. Let's say you are managing a telephone-based team and, typically, that team answers 92 percent of its calls every day. OK, sometimes it's 91 percent or 90 percent or maybe 93 percent, but it averages out quite nicely at 92 percent. One day you come in and see that the answer rate yesterday was 74 percent. What do you do?

Wrong, you don't bring a baseball bat into a meeting of team managers. Wrong, you don't immediately telephone HR and ask for 12 new people. Wrong, you don't call the team managers and ask them what happened (even if that sounds logical).

But if you don't do any of those things, what do you do?

You start by calmly checking to make sure that the 74 percent number is correct. What if the phone system had a problem after 6 pm yesterday and was registering calls that couldn't be answered? Or what if the data feed in the morning was missing information from somewhere and was just plain wrong?

Whatever, the first thing you always do is verify the data. I have an embarrassing story to tell in this regard. An event that taught me: Look before you leap!

This goes back to when I was managing the marketing and sales teams in Chicago. I was still in my twenties and thought that, as the manager, I had to show that I was in charge. One day the office assistant, a very nice lady called Melody, was late. She was supposed to start at 9.15 and she wasn't there at 9.30. Or 9.45. She finally came in a few minutes before 10.

She didn't say anything to anyone and just settled into her chair. I came over to her desk and in a loud voice, to ensure that everyone in the office could hear me, asked, "Where have you been?" She looked up at me with a strange expression and hesitated. So, naturally, I repeated my question. I might have even increased the volume a tad to make sure everyone knew who was in charge. This time she just nodded her head as if she had no choice and said, "I've been out shopping for your birthday gift on behalf of everyone in the office."

Oops.

When I moved into marketing and sales at the futures broker-age firm, I wondered which of our customers were generating the most revenue. I started adding up a couple of weeks' worth of trading. I was stunned to find that a very small number of cus-tomers were generating more than half our revenue.

It was really basic info that jumped off the page. But nobody had done this simple analysis before. And because of that we were treating every customer in exactly the same way. Once we identified the small number of lucrative customers, we installed a special phone number that had priority over all the other lines, and only gave this number to those big traders.

Here's how to outperform the competition: Be more thorough in data collection and cleverer in data interrogation. See things the others don't.

You'd be surprised at the data some firms don't collect. When I was at Churchill, the CEO decided that because drivers under the age of 25 were producing poor results, we wouldn't even quote for them. This is quite different to only offering very high premiums. If you go ahead and offer high premiums, you'll see what the market might support via the movement in your conversion rate. But if you don't offer them quotes at all you never get the data. You're in the dark.

Sometimes there is less-obvious data that is worth collecting. For example: How long has a customer been driving? If you've held your license for three years or less, Admiral wants to know exactly how many months. Both 15 months and nine months could be rounded off to one year. But someone with 15 months has 66 percent more experience than someone with nine months.

There's a cross-subsidy between people with nine months' experience and those with 15. Admiral can price with greater precision by charging the customer with nine months a bit more and the one with 15 months a bit less. Firms that only collect data in "year" chunks will attract more of the nine-monthers and fewer of the 15-monthers. And their results for one-year license holders will get worse because they have more drivers with less experience. Then they'll raise their rates accordingly.

When they do that, they've just made it even easier for Admiral to land the 15-monthers and possibly to get the nine-monthers at a profitable rate.

Like so many things in management, measuring data is an acquired skill. The more of it you do, the better you'll be at doing it.

CHAPTER 19

THE "NOT BAD" TRAP

Much of the time, managers are trying to turn chaos into order. That's the way businesses are. We talk in terms of "trying to get things to run smoothly" and "avoid firefighting." Managers want today to be a bit better than yesterday and tomorrow a bit better again; they want incremental improvement without any shocks to the system.

That's why we often just ask for "exception reporting." We want to see the areas that are not normal. Makes sense, right? If you convert 20 percent of leads to customers every day for two years and then one week it falls to 15 percent, you need to react, right? But if it stayed at 20 percent, well, why bother looking at it? We were happy with 20 percent yesterday so no reason we shouldn't be happy today. That's both an intelligent way to manage and part of the problem. When numbers don't change, it fills managers with self-satisfaction and inhibits them from thinking how they can make significant improvement. That's human nature, but it's not the best way to run a business.

I recently gave a talk to Admiral managers and asked what the overall attrition rate was for staff. They said something like 25 percent. They were pretty pleased with that. And in truth, that's a pretty good number for a big company with a very large telephone-based workforce.

I'm sure if the managers were targeted to reach 23 percent or 24 percent they could make a few tweaks and hit that target. They would look for a couple of quick wins, perhaps ensure only the best people did the actual recruiting and, voilà, it wouldn't take much to knock off a point or so, at least temporarily.

Then I challenged them: "What if no one in this room would get any shares or bonus money unless the overall attrition rate were 5 percent? What would you do then?" They looked at me like I should be wearing a straitjacket.

But putting an impossible number in front of someone means rethinking everything. For attrition, it isn't just about the recruitment. It starts with the image the company has in the community. How the job is advertised. The recruitment and interview process. The financial package offered. All the other things offered that attract people.

After they arrive, there is the first-day indoctrination and that all-important first week with the company. Then the training program. Then the job they actually have to do. Then the daily motivation from their team manager. You see where this is going? Taking the target out of the comfort zone forces managers to rethink every step of the process. It is no longer about a quick win—it's about a thorough review to create fundamental change.

This brings up an important related topic: false economies. It's a very tempting trap, especially for the people entrusted with a company's bottom line. We've all seen this happen.

There are times when the Finance department, fretting about costs, will send around a memo saying that all budgets have to be reduced by, say, 10 percent. This happens in a lot of businesses. Managers naturally turn to variable costs to achieve the goal. And those variable costs often mean people. They reason that either their people are overpaid or that there are too many of them.

In some instances, this line of reasoning might be correct. However, often it leads to a false economy and poorer results. Let me explain how.

Let's take the attrition situation. Why would I advocate an attrition rate so insanely low? The value is obvious: Experienced people are more efficient and give better service to customers (external and internal). And that leads to more income. The cost: Experienced workers are paid more.

But when that cost-cutting memo comes around, many managers reason that if they replace some people who have been with the company for a few years with new, lower-salaried people, they'll hit that 10 percent reduction number.

As I said, this is tempting. But hold the bus. Before you do this, take a good look and try to measure the value of experience. As discussed in the previous chapter, try to measure everything. This can be difficult, but it's important. Look at everything you possibly can:

- How much output do you get from someone with six months' experience versus two years?
- How many customers per day does each group handle?
- How much management time is spent with those two

groups? (An extra, but slightly hidden, cost, since the managers are paid anyway. But, hey, maybe the key is fewer managers?)

- How many first-touch resolutions are there?
- Can you measure customer satisfaction and tie that back to the agent involved?

In addition to these probing, specific questions, keep the big picture in mind: In our business renewals are of great importance. Again (as almost always!) it helps to look at this from a customer's point of view. A lot of factors lead to her decision to renew or not. Certainly there's the price. But even the price is going to be affected by how the customer has been treated since she was first prompted to contact the company, all the way through to getting the notice of renewal. A call two weeks ago might have more influence on her than a call a year ago, but everything is in the hopper.

Think about the customer's thresholds. The first threshold is how much effort she will put into shopping. If she is not happy with the service or price she's received over the period, she is likely to put a lot of effort into finding a better offer. The more effort she puts in, the more likely she is to find a better deal and move on.

Second threshold is how big a price difference it would take to get her to move. If the service has been horrible she'll probably jump to another firm even if it charges £50 more. But if the service and reputation of the company are good then this threshold is lowered and generally goes the other way—that is, the competition has to be £25 or £50 or maybe even £100 cheaper to get the customer to switch. The better the experience, the higher her threshold for leaving. The ultimate is no shopping, just renewing.

The point is, experienced staff are likely to give customers that better impression. They are less likely to put customers on hold, less likely to have to ask a manager to get something done. They are more likely to sort things out quickly, the first time a customer makes contact. Good service leads to more renewals.

Unfortunately, many managers are managing only a particular segment of the business and don't always have the big picture in view. Their ostensibly rational reaction would be to take the action that makes their numbers look good, even if that's not optimal for the company as a whole.

So that cost-cutting memo might lead to poorer service and fewer renewals, or lower prices (and margins) to keep the business. It also is likely to lead to fewer sales of other products and services, which are typically lucrative sales because the marketing cost has already been spent on the core product. (Companies known for great service can sell almost anything to their customers.)

But you, the manager, are still stuck with this memo from Finance. What do you do? First, do nothing—step back and think a bit. Don't just dive right in looking for places to cut.

What knowledge would be valuable to you? In this example, I'd want to know how important staff experience is to customer satisfaction. What changes in behavior would improve that satisfaction? Get creative in your thinking.

You might end up with a counter-intuitive proposal: Give a raise to all staff with more than one year's experience. This will keep more of them in the company, doing the jobs that need to be done. The upshot could be more income. The Finance department might baulk at raises, but they'd love the idea of more income. That's the other side of the "reduce expenses" coin. Truth is, the Finance department doesn't really care if it's more income per pound spent or less money spent per pound of income. Sadly, it's easier to assess the latter than the former. It would be unusual to get a memo from Finance saying everyone had to increase turnover by 10 percent! Good managers must challenge this. Good managers must think about cutbacks, sure, but they must also think about the other side of that coin. Try to think differently.

So, good luck with that idea of giving raises to save money! Let me know how that works out. Let's move on.

As I said at the beginning of this chapter, it's easy for managers to get comfortable with their numbers. Especially those that don't move very much or very often (numbers, not managers). We all do. But this smooth sailing means we lose the initiative to think radically and make positive changes. There's another saying from American football: If you're not getting better, you're getting worse. This implies that your competitors are not being complacent, so you'd better not be, either.

Only by challenging people, taking them well away from their comfort zones, do you get the thinking that's needed to move ahead. If you throw out a number to challenge your audience and they don't sputter, "That's impossible," then you haven't hit it hard enough.

Here's another example, which I use in training sessions. In one of our businesses we have a conversion rate of 25 percent. People are pretty happy with that. One in four; not bad.

But I look at that and say, "Wait—that means 75 of 100 people who contact us *do not* buy. Holy cow! How can that be? What happens to them?"

I mean that literally: What happens to those 75 people? They are so interested in buying that they contact us! But then they bugger off without buying. Let's find out. Let's look at each and every one of them and find out where they went, where they took their business, what they thought of our offer.

When we do this, we find the answers for why 30 or even 40 customers of the 75 don't buy. But that leaves 35 unaccounted for! Thirty-five of 100 where we didn't understand why they weren't buying! What an opportunity!

"Why isn't our conversion rate 85 percent?" I ask.

Again, if we challenge the managers to move conversion from 25 percent to 27 percent, I suspect they can do it by launching a bonus program or increasing incentives in some way. There are ways to get a bit more energy on the sales. But if they are challenged to go to 85 percent the managers are going to do a whole lot of work—a lot of creative thinking—to understand what's going on in their business.

These examples are often for telephone-based departments. But the concept goes everywhere, any business, any department.

When you're looking at your numbers, you will naturally tend to focus on those that are out of sync. But greatness doesn't come from moving from 25 percent to 27 percent. Don't get me wrong, it's not bad to improve, even if the improvement is modest. I'm all for it. Greatness, however, comes from reaching for 85 percent. Notice I said "reaching for," not "reaching." You might never get to 85 percent but even if you "only" move it to 45 percent, it would be a significant improvement.

You probably know the concept of "kaizen," or continuous daily improvement, adopted in post-war Japan. As I said, that's great. But it's easy to fall into the "incremental improvement" trap where you can see the progress.

Guess what? You can do both. Incremental improvement is not mutually exclusive to significant improvement. It's just that significant change takes a lot more energy and thought to achieve.

It also means you have to be able to think outside the proverbial box more.

Here's what I love about striving for significant change: You first have to take something apart to see how it works, and you'll naturally understand it better. You can't help but learn when you take a process apart, brick by brick, and reassemble it in a better way. This knowledge is sure to be helpful in the future, well beyond any individual initiative.

My recommendation? Every month (or even more frequently) take one of your metrics, look at it and put a very different, new number on it. Go to your business model and put the new number into your plan. I suspect you'll be amazed at what that single significant change does to the results popping out at the bottom of the model.

If the improvement to the bottom line blows you away, trust me, it's worth a little extra effort to figure out how to make it happen.

Greater expectations

- When challenging a team, go big.
- Question all aspects of an operation.
- Remember the customer.
- Don't get comfortable—with numbers or procedures.
- Greatness comes from reaching.
- Plug in a new number and see what would happen.
- Then make it happen.

CHAPTER 20

WE'RE ALWAYS NEGOTIATING

When you and your partner are trying to decide what show to watch in the evening or where to go for dinner, you are negotiating. When you want the board of directors to increase your budget, you are negotiating. When you want a bit of extra effort from your team, you are negotiating. And on and on.

Think about your own experiences for a moment. Think of a good negotiation, personal or professional. What made it good? How did it work?

Now think of a bad negotiation. Why was it bad? What happened that made it bad or not work?

Take a moment and write down what made those negotiations work and not work. Then see if what you jotted down is similar to my list.

THE PRACTICAL

Four keys to negotiation

- Information is king.
- Think like the other side.
- Set parameters for yourself and the other side.
- Time.

In a negotiation, information really is power. It's simple: If you're buying a house, it helps to know why the seller is selling. Is it a couple who are moving but under no time pressure? Or is it a divorce where both people have to find their own place—now! If so, a lower offer might be accepted. An older couple with no deadline are likely to wait longer to get their number. You've already hit three of the four keys above: You have info, you know how they're thinking, and you've factored time into your playbook.

Negotiation isn't easy but it also isn't rocket science. If you're buying a car, for instance, and know that bonuses are paid to salespeople at the end of the month, you'll probably get the best deal then.

Decades ago, when my wife and I were backpacking in Asia, we'd read that in Indonesia—where everything is negotiated—the merchants often give a better discount to make their first sale of the day. Makes sense, as a way to get the day going.

So we were in a market and saw something we liked, and started bargaining. But we didn't buy it, thinking we might be able to find it cheaper elsewhere during the day. Well, we didn't. In the late afternoon we went back to the original merchant but the price had changed. No longer were we eligible for the "first sale of the day discount," and we were leaving the next morning. If only we had trusted the information we had and hadn't assumed it was a standard negotiation.

Another negotiating superpower is the ability to think like the other side. But we're not superhuman and usually only think like ourselves. We don't really know what is making the other side tick. If we did, we might find out that the other side puts a greater value on things that we don't value very highly.

I did many negotiations at Admiral with reinsurers. I came to understand that reinsurers put a very high value on volume in a relatively low volatility business, like car insurance. It makes sense, right? So much of their portfolio was made up of low-probability/high-severity events—things like earthquakes in California. They might go a year or longer when there was no earthquake damage, and they would clean up. But one good shake could cost them a fortune! The loss ratio spread might go from 0 percent to 1,000 percent and more.

Along comes a motor insurer, whose results are reliably between 95 percent and 105 percent. This is pretty stable stuff and helps them balance their portfolio. That's valuable to them. It's also sizeable income, which helps cover their overheads and feed their investment divisions. Understanding this, we were then able to do deals where both parties got more of what they wanted.

We were interested in absolute profit, so profit commissions on their share of the profits were of particular importance to us. They valued the volume (money they could invest and earn a return on) and stability and were a bit less interested in absolute profit. In fact, we didn't want the volume, because it would require us to put up more capital, while they had excess capital, which they were keen to put to work. They also had a lower cost of capital, so their return on capital of £1 of profit was greater than ours. In the negotiation it seemed a bit counter-intuitive because of the increased risk, but we would offer them more volume in return for us getting a greater percentage of their profits, which they thought was OK. The proverbial win-win!

Setting parameters for yourself—and even for the other side—can be crucial. Among the worst of my negotiations were those where I set myself a line in the sand and then stepped across it. There's an old adage in negotiation: If they move once, they'll move again. It's not an old adage for nothing! I've had investments that needed more funding, even though I had previously said I would not add to the investment. But of course when push came to shove, I did add to the investment.

No biggie if it's one time and the money was needed, right? Except for this: The other side never believed me again when I said, "No more."

Don't set parameters that you can't adhere to. If at all possible, know your limits when you go into a negotiation and try to figure out the other side's limits. Those are three of the keys right there: knowledge, thinking like the other side, and setting parameters.

Have you ever been to an Egyptian or Turkish bazaar? If you want to learn the art of negotiation, spend an hour or two there! You walk past an old gentleman sipping tea in front of a stack of backgammon sets. All very nice wood. You slow down to look. He's locking in to his target. You pick one up to examine it more closely. Bingo! He knows he's got a fish on the line.

Of course, there are no price tags on these items. You show it to your partner. The seller licks his chops. "Hand-carved," he coos, "finest beechwood, inlaid mother-of-pearl." It doesn't look that exceptional, but what do you know? You take the plunge. "How much?" He gives you a figure in local currency, and your mental conversion arrives at £180. Gulp. That seems a lot. It is quite nice and would be an excellent souvenir. But that does seem high.

Freeze frame! What should you do at this point? Look around: He has a hundred of these sets. And the guy just up the walk has another hundred. Then figure what price you'd want to pay for this. Maybe £20. So, the right thing to do is offer him £15, hoping to compromise at £20. But what do we do? We think that such an offer would be insulting. If you said, "I'll give you 15 quid for it," you might look stupid. So you probably mumble something like, "That seems a bit high." He tells you again of the virtues of this backgammon set. But then he says, "Tell me, my friend, how much would you pay for it?"

It probably cost him £5 and if he got £20 for it he'd be a happy camper. This does not diminish his enthusiasm for trying to get you to pay in excess of £100 for it. So now he is asking you to set a floor on the negotiation. If you're smart you say £5 and don't care if he's insulted. Because if you go much higher he's going to reel you in.

You could just say, "That's too expensive," and start to walk away. Let him come back with a lower ceiling rather than you establishing the floor. And if he moves by more than £5 then you know he's playing you and that he'll move again and again to make the sale.

In the end you might beat him down to £80 and feel that you got it for less than half price. But this isn't the Christmas sales at your local department store. This is an item for which you had far less information than he had—you don't really know what such a backgammon set can be made for or purchased for. You're not even sure what mother-of-pearl is.

The smart shopper walks away from the first two or three salesmen and builds his information base on asking prices and possible reductions. But you don't have the time for research and bargaining; you're on a sightseeing holiday. You can't set parameters because of your understandable ignorance. And it's hard to think like him because, face it, his life is nothing like yours.

The result? He's got you on information, as he knows his costs and margins, and he's got you on time, because he's going to sit there all day and do nothing else but drink tea and sell backgammon sets.

My advice: Give up and buy the damned backgammon set and enjoy it as a treasure from an exotic holiday every time you play!

But my points stand regarding business negotiations: Know as much as you can before you start and remember that people who do something for a living have a big advantage over you if you're just negotiating on this one occasion. Don't be arrogant and think you can know more than they do.

My fourth point is the value of time. It's similar to recruiting—if you can give yourself unlimited time, you'll do a lot better. That's rare, though.

I have a friend in commercial real estate. He had an apartment building he was selling and he either had to sell it or remortgage it. He had an acceptable deal for the sale going through and so had the remortgage on the back burner. Of course—or this wouldn't be much of a story—the sale fell through at the last hurdle and he was forced to remortgage.

The bank doing the remortgage smelled his time deadline like a hungry fox smells a baby rabbit. They added extra clauses and charges and made it a pretty poor deal for him. But he had to do it. He got stuck by time. The only option would have been to run two parties to the end on the sale, hoping one would make it to the end, while simultaneously running two parties to the end on the remortgage just in case the building didn't sell. (This, of course, would have been exhausting. But it would have ensured that he could play one off the other in both scenarios rather than getting stuck into either taking a very unattractive offer or a bad remortgage.) At the other end, if you can find out the time pressures on the other side, be they end-of-year sales quotas or somebody hungrier than you and therefore more likely to accept your choice of restaurant, then you can control the negotiation.

What about tactics? Here are four different tactics for negotiating:

1. Play it straight.
2. Bluff!
3. Ask for more, settle for less.
4. Move the goalposts.

First, *play it straight*. That's right: Be honest, tell the other side what you want and what you're willing to give for it. This is generally how we negotiate in our personal lives (right?), but it can also be very effective in a work context. Funny how people often respect honesty! (It's so rare that it's often modified with the adjective "refreshing.")

The opposite is to *bluff*! Remember, the other side doesn't know exactly what your situation is. So try to fool them. If you're selling your house, make it seem like you couldn't care less if you sell tomorrow or in six months—even if you desperately need the money next Thursday!

We see this all the time in Admiral with exaggerated injury claims. I remember one claimant was asking for a large sum because he couldn't use his arm anymore. We had a private investigator join the guy's archery club and surreptitiously video-tape him with a huge bow snug on his shoulder, using a lot of force to pull the bowstring back and releasing it at the target. He was a good shot. When we showed his solicitor the video, the claim went away.

That is, of course, the downside of the bluff. If someone finds out you're bluffing it might cost you a lot. If the claimant, who clearly was not really injured, had asked for less we might not have thought it worth investigating and he would have received something for his fraudulent efforts.

In most normal situations, however, I'd recommend you *ask for more*, knowing that you'll compromise for less. But the "less" is actually your target—your parameter. I told you how my old boss, Herb, went into a meeting and asked that we cut out all the advertising and then, after much wrangling, we'd settle on a cut of $50,000 or $100,000. What did Herb really want? I don't know, but I doubt he really wanted us to discontinue advertising. And, funny, but he seemed quite content with the reduction! (Bluff!)

My favorite technique is *moving the goalposts*. So, when the guy in the Egyptian bazaar offers you a backgammon set for £180, ask him for two backgammon sets and two shisha pipes for £180. And don't forget to get a cup of tea as well.

If you're not happy with the deal on the table then stretch it out and bring other things into play. Some of our reinsurance negotiations were almost comical in the way that they started with a simple renegotiation of one country for three years and ended up as a five-country, multi-year deal! We just kept throwing in something else to try to get a better deal and then they'd come back and say, "Well, if you want that and that, we'd like this and this." Well, if they wanted this and this, then we wanted this, that, and the other!

Often by moving the goalposts you can add exchanges to the core deal, where the extra items you're giving have less value to you than they do to the other side, and vice versa.

*

WE'RE ALWAYS NEGOTIATING

Well, that's it. We've covered a lot of ground in Part 4 on the practical world of leading a team, running an office, training and inspiring, hiring and firing, making deals and taking lunches. But hang on—let me offer a bit more on the less practical but (I'd argue) more important side of leadership and management. It's about you and the team and, well, gratitude.

And it won't cost you anything more!

Bargaining points

- Know your facts—and the other side.
- Set a number and stick to it.
- Don't rush. If you are rushed, don't let on.
- Honesty is the best way.
- Except when bluffing is.
- Ask for Jupiter; you might get Saturn.
- Get creative and see what happens.

PART 5

CONCLUSION

CHAPTER 21

WELCOMES AND FAREWELLS

It was after midnight and we were tired and disappointed. Then the bus driver got lost. Remember when I wrote that the route to Admiral's success wasn't one nice, long yellow brick road? In this case, we couldn't even find the road!

We had just finished a particularly disappointing night at a Best Companies to Work For dinner and ceremony in London. It was late and we had finished 30-somethingth in the list. As if to match our mood, the bus driver then lost his way trying to exit London. Oof.

As tired as we were, though, the 10 of us on the bus spent much of the ride trying to figure out ways we could do better. The 10 people were from all over the company, almost every department represented and all different levels. What could we do within the organisation, departments, and teams to promote better welfare?

CONCLUSION

If we could identify our weak spots, presumably we'd eventually get a better score on the comprehensive staff questionnaire that determined the awards. Getting a better score would indicate that we were engaging better with our staff and the upshot of that should be better results!

By the time we neared Cardiff, the discussion had died down and many had drifted into sleep. But I was really moved by how much the people on that bus wanted to do better. So, I started to think: How could we get everyone at Admiral to be like that? To have such a desire to do better?

And that's when it hit me: Why don't we do our own Best Department to Work For in Admiral competition? Take the motivation of these people on the bus and turn it loose on the company. With an internal competition, we could inspire each department to look for ways it could improve.

We did the first one in 2005, and it was brilliant. We borrowed the system used by the outside contests: Send a questionnaire around to staff and use those scores to calculate each department's grade. We improved it over the years, adding site visits and then a presentation by each department to a panel of judges. Everyone was so keen to win!

But the idea wasn't to have one really happy department and everyone else depressed. We wanted the departments that didn't win to work harder so they could win the following year. There were some disappointed people after that first event, to be sure, but by and large everyone took it on board to work harder so they could win the following year. We made sure that all the feedback we received that led to each department's score was fed back to the leadership of that department. We also encouraged them to talk with or go see what the winning departments were doing. We wanted to create an atmosphere of continuous improvement.

Some years ago we expanded it to include all non-UK operations. The award ceremony is a fantastic evening. We host a black-tie dinner in Cardiff and fill the hall with 400 staff. Every business and every large department is represented. It's one of the best evenings of the year. Everyone is dressed to the nines and keen as mustard to win. There's a table from Spain, others from Italy, Halifax and Delhi, several from Swansea, many from Cardiff.

Here's the beautiful part: It's not an event for managers. Some managers attend, yes, but most of the audience is made up of people from the department, chosen by performance or random draw. It's a great way to pull people from throughout the organisation—some from thousands of miles away—to spend a week at HQ. For some of these people it is the first time they have ever travelled abroad.

There are awards by size of department and also some individual honors. The climax is the countdown of the Top 10 Call Center Departments. The atmosphere is electric as we get to those final spots and slowly, teasingly, announce the winner. It's a glorious event, a true celebration of our people—and of our devotion to continual improvement.

Besides that, we gather a lot of useful data. We get detailed numbers for all the departments, across all questions, divided by a variety of demographics.

As usual, measurement is key. As noted above, after the event the judges give detailed feedback to every department with a thorough review of all the data, showing which questions the department scored well on and which they did less well on. If a department scores poorly several years in a row, the discussions about remedial actions are more directive.

The presentations to the judges that I mentioned are amazing team-builders. Most departments go to great lengths to do a brilliant presentation, often resulting in a performance by more than 100 people—usually in costume, dancing and singing to newly minted lyrics that address the theme the judges have put forth.

Each department produces a short paper on the theme, which in the past have included:

- There is only one share price—how do you share excellence across the Group?
- How do you ensure that a culture of positive change and continuous improvement exists within your department?
- Admiral does not believe in creating individual stars but strongly believes that the team is greater than an individual. How does your department's style of leadership make sure the team is always at the front?
- As the business continues to grow, how do you ensure that every member of staff continues to feel like a key piece in the Admiral Group puzzle?
- Admiral being different to the market is part of our DNA and a source of competitive advantage. How is your department different?

Admiral's Top 10 has been an unqualified success. It's a great source of pride for the winners and motivation for the rest. The energy that goes into trying to win is energy well spent creating a better organisation with highly motivated people. At the core of this success are four things that always play a big role in Admiral: measurement, creativity, inspiration, and the never-ending desire to improve results. We've managed to combine constructive change with great fun!

When I watch the staff working together in friendly competition, I can't help but think back to those Welcome Talks I gave to every one of them. I gave the talk to nearly 20,000 people over a quarter of a century. And at every one, I'd give each person a piece of a jigsaw puzzle as they sat down.

When I got to a certain point in my talk I would ask them to look at their puzzle piece and tell me what the picture of the puzzle was. Of course, no one ever could. Simple message: You can't look at a single piece and see the picture; no individual makes the puzzle. The only way you can see the whole picture is to put the pieces together—to work together.

What we were looking for, I told these new employees, were team players; people who wanted to help each other. We didn't want solitary heroes—we weren't looking for John Wayne to jump out of the foxhole and mow down the enemy. (Later on, when I realised my audience didn't have a clue who John Wayne was, I was obliged to change it to Brad Pitt.)

I told them that we were all here for the same thing: the success of this company. With that in mind, we needed to work together, which included asking for help when it was needed. I told them that in too many organisations people were afraid to put up their hand if they needed help. They fear people will think they're stupid and that they will maybe get fired. But in Admiral, I said, if you don't put up your hand to get help and then do something wrong, that's when we think you're stupid and fire you. I told them that was a joke. Sort of.

This principle works up, down, and sideways. I'd tell them they should not only expect help from their managers and trainers but they should get used to helping each other. I would point to two people in the audience and say I was sure there were some things the person on the left did better than the person on the right. "So help her!" I'd say, then point to the person on the right. "And I'm certain there are things you do better than him, so help him out!"

The power of the team is invariably greater than the power of any single individual. Teamwork makes for better outcomes.

Here's something I said earlier, but it still might surprise you: Winning as a team is a far greater pleasure than winning as an individual. We're raised in societies where there are winners and losers and we're taught at an early age that it's better to be a winner than a loser. And even low-ego people want to succeed in their own right and for their own benefit. That's fine. But winning as a team brings a good feeling that far surpasses individual achievement.

I remember the first time we won Welsh Company of the Year back in the late 1990s. It was all part of a somewhat new awards programme. The previous year we had been short-listed for the top prize but, amazing to us, we didn't win. We went back again the following year and we were a nervous table all night waiting for the result. And when they announced that we'd won, we were beside ourselves. We'd done it. We'd succeeded. We were the best. The pride we all felt in that accomplishment, as a team, was immense.

Anybody who has played a team sport knows this, has felt this. The Team, the Team, the Team.

When I retired from Admiral my wife and I gave a gift of £1,000 to every member of staff with more than one year's service (and £500 to those who'd started more recently). Some 8,000 people. We did this because these were the people who—along with a few thousand others who had come and gone in 25-plus years— played, and are playing, a big role in the success of our company. We wanted to say, "Thanks, we're all winners here." We wanted to celebrate my (semi-)retirement with everyone in the company because it was only together that we were able to build a company as successful as Admiral Group.

We had some great moments in building Admiral. I'll never forget one London meeting in particular.

Our Lloyd's of London parent company had been bought out by a Bermudan reinsurer. The Bermudans wanted to convince our direct parent company that we should not be part of their future. To do this work they engaged McKinsey, the management consultants, basically to do a hatchet job on us. They planned to use McKinsey's research as a battering ram to convince our direct parent to sell us (this being the same parent company we'd been fighting for several years).

Of course, that's not what they told us to our faces! They told us they had asked McKinsey in to review the car insurance business in general and ourselves and our sister car insurer in the Group (which operated through brokers). But, weirdly, soon after McKinsey started, they no longer spent any time with the sister company. And when it came time for the presentation meeting, we could smell what was in the offing.

David and I went to the London meeting well prepared. Pro tip: Go to a meeting really well prepared and it has a chance to be one of the greatest meetings you'll ever be in.

We watched as these very expensive consultants presented slide after slide to make their case. McKinsey said we were sub-scale and that anything we had achieved that was superior to the market would be competed away in short order. All very logical and all very wrong.

Then it was our turn. We were in the boardroom and there were about 10 people around the table. There were three or four people from our immediate parent company, one from the parent company's parent company, at least two people from McKinsey,

David and myself. We had been building towards this moment for months, ever since we were told McKinsey would give us some "help". I can't remember if I was smiling as David and I began, but I was, shall we say, feeling confident. We were ready.

We destroyed everything McKinsey had put forward. We turned every argument they made against them. We patiently explained that even at our current size our economics were superior to the market and profitable even in difficult market conditions. They claimed all the income we received from selling other products to our customers would be competed away. We calmly explained why consumers don't buy those products on price, as they do for car insurance, and, as such, these products produce a much less volatile stream of earnings. They claimed we were sub-scale and so couldn't compete with bigger competitors. We countered by showing that our results were already superior to those of bigger competitors, even though we were small. And as we grew and gained economies of scale our results would become even better.

You get the picture. We finished and there were just a few questions. As soon as they could, the McKinsey folks made a beeline for the exit.

Looking back, this meeting is even sweeter than it was on the day (and it was pretty sweet on the day!) because pretty much everything we claimed then was proved correct over time.

(But such is life: As you already know, the parent company's parent company still put us up for sale, saying we weren't core!)

That David and I did this meeting together made it a far sweeter triumph than if either of us had done it individually. And we knew it was a true team effort—we had all the data we needed from around the company, the result of a lot of hard graft put in by our colleagues and staff.

David and I have done a lot of meetings together and instinctively we knew when one of us needed a hand, when it was the right time to push back against the other side, when we should add a detail, etc. Basically, we knew how to support each other.

We had a lot of good laughs that evening on the train from London back to Cardiff and it was great the next day when we got the managers together and told them what had happened.

Not only is it better to win as a team but being a team even makes losing easier. As the saying goes, misery loves company. When you lose as a team, you can lean on each other, laugh it off together, and regroup, knowing that there are others who have your back.

Enough about the ancient past. Let's jump ahead more than 20 years, to 2017, and Elephant, and then look into the future. Don't worry, this isn't turning into science fiction. In fact, I'm still on the age-old principle of teamwork.

It's key to get people involved in your business. When people are involved they do more, care more, deliver more. Further, the extra knowledge everyone in the company has about how the company runs will be a benefit. So get them involved in various aspects of the business.

One obvious benefit is the ability to move people from one area to another without too much hassle. People in one area can help those in another area if they know how that other area works. Maybe one department does something that another department can learn from. If it works in one office, maybe it'll work in another.

When I went in as CEO of Elephant in 2017 the first thing I did was try to get all the managers in the organisation involved in the company's future. At the time Elephant had about 550 staff and about 100 managers or equivalents. In the talk I gave to managers that first morning, I announced a new initiative.

CONCLUSION

I asked the managers for volunteers to create a new business plan for Elephant. I was convinced the company's current plan was not taking the company forward and I had recent results to back this up. I knew we needed a new plan. And I thought the managers might appreciate being given a chance to have some input into this new plan.

I thought we might get 30 or so volunteers and we'd have four or five teams. We got 96 volunteers! We had 11 teams and each one did the work, much of it in their own time, to create a new business plan. I gave them two months to come up with a plan and only pocket money for research. If they wanted to do more research they had to use staff or friends and family, which wouldn't cost anything.

Sure, some of the people dropped off along the way, but most stayed through to the presentations. We did feedback on the whole exercise afterwards. It was gratifying to see that most people said the two biggest benefits were 1) working with people they normally wouldn't work with or didn't know; and 2) learning about how the whole business hangs together.

From these 11 teams we chose the four best plans, consolidated some of the teams, and thanked the others for their help. We then had those four teams do more research (spend money!) on their ideas and then those four teams presented their findings to the Elephant board. We took three of the plans, condensed them into one, and started changing the business accordingly. Every person who worked on those plans came away feeling they had a bigger stake in the company's future. That can only work to our advantage.

Now when managers are trying to dream up ideas on any subject I am quick to recommend that they open it out to a large group, break into teams (side benefit: Give team leadership not to your top managers but to your prospective managers and see how they get on), and let many people get involved.

Of course it's not all about the Team, the Team, the… you get it.

It's also about you.

Are you a talented person? In any way, shape, or form? I'm not looking for Olympic gold, just whether you think you have any talent whatsoever. If you can answer yes to this question, which you should be able to do, then I have another question for you. It has nothing to do with your work but one you should ask yourself on a regular basis, no matter where you are and what you're doing, and the question is:

What are you doing to make the most of your talent?

I'd like you to pay particular attention to two words in that sentence: *you* and *doing*.

This is about you, not the team around you. You all said you're talented, right? What are *you doing* with that talent? Are you growing it, cultivating it, nurturing it? Or is it like water, just slipping through your fingers?

As for the "you" part, I don't mean what is being done to you, at you, with you, or for you. I mean what are *you* actually doing to be better? Please don't answer that you come to work each day and therefore you'll get better. That's not really an overt action you are taking to improve. Think about it. You have talent, natural ability. We all do. It's what we do with it that makes the difference. *What are you doing with yours?*

I want to end this book the way I like to end meetings: on an upbeat note.

We tend to take a lot of things for granted in life. But if someone asked you, "What are you grateful for?" I'm sure you could come up with a long list. A number of years ago I heard a speaker suggest doing "gratefuls" every morning with your family. Here's how it works: Each morning you each say something you're grateful for and add them to your master list of gratefuls. Every day everyone is supposed to bring new gratefuls to the table. My wife, youngest daughter, and I did this for a while at home and found it was quite a nice way to begin the day. Now we're empty nesters but my wife and I still try to do this most mornings.

When I got to Elephant in 2017, I knew I had to do radical surgery on the culture. People were down, they were closed-up, they didn't work together, and they didn't try to get to know their fellow managers.

Right away I introduced that 8.45 am meeting for senior managers, which slowly grew from six or seven people to as many as 30 on some days. People were now talking to each other and learning from each other. A good start.

Almost 30 years ago we began a small initiative to help Admiral managers make the most of their talent. It's called the Admiral Book Scheme. If any member of staff wants to buy, within a reasonable cost, a book, DVD, app, whatever, that will help them do their job better, the company will gladly pay for it. Many hundreds of staff have used the scheme since its inception and to date Admiral has spent over £1 million. And it's spending more all the time. Programs like this make it easier for people to get the most from their natural ability.

Then I decided we could all use some gratefulness. At the end of every meeting, I proposed, we should go around the circle so everyone could say one thing they were grateful for. They would try not to repeat that "grateful" in future days. (For instance, today I could say coffee and you could say sunshine but tomorrow I couldn't say coffee again, but I could say sunshine.)

On big-group days this could take 10 minutes or more. Earnest? Yeah, a little. But nobody rolled their eyes and everyone bought into it. I think they wanted this outlet—they wanted permission to express gratitude for certain things or people. It's kind of a rare thing in business.

This meant the meeting always ended on a positive note, which was a great thing for morale and productivity. Everyone is upbeat, thinking about what they're grateful for and hearing what others are grateful for. During the day, invariably you'd see something that you are grateful for—maybe the sunset or a kind gesture among team members—and you'd note it, rather than just letting it wash over you. You know you'll use it the following morning.

It is a constant reminder that we all have so much to be grateful for. It also teaches you about your peers. Some people around the circle would always be grateful for their children, for others it was nature, and for others it was the dog, or how nice the in-laws were, or partners. Others were grateful for people in the office who worked extra hard or delivered projects on time. It was a great way to learn about your teammates.

As far as I know, they are still doing this at Elephant today, many years later, and other parts of the group have started doing it as well.

I have enough things to be grateful for to last me a couple of lifetimes of morning meetings. I am hugely grateful to have worked with so many fantastic people. People who were committed to doing their best and working together as a team. I believe I can speak for all of these people when I say that we are proud not only to have created such a successful business in a commodity-like industry but proud of the way we did it—and I'm proud to say that Admiral still does it, every day.

Many books start with a quote that only makes sense after you've read the book. I'd prefer to leave you with one.

It's my favorite business quote. It was written about entrepreneurs, but it applies to anyone who loves being in business and management. It was written by an economist from the first part of the 20th century, Joseph Schumpeter:

> *"There is the will to conquer: the impulse to fight, to prove oneself superior to others, to succeed for the sake, not of the fruits of success, but of success itself... Finally, there is the joy of creating, of getting things done, or simply exercising one's energy and ingenuity."*

That says it all. Get out there and succeed, be great, because you can. It's not about what you'll get if you're great, it's about being great because not everyone is... but you can be.

Leadership and management are hard work. Understatement of the book! But they can also be hugely rewarding because you have the opportunity to change people's lives for the better. Can you have a better job than that?

Think about it.

YOUR ULTIMATE CHECKLIST

I've thrown a lot of tips at you in this book. Looking back, these are the top eight I'd like you to remember:

1

If people like what they do, they'll do it better.

2

The Team, the Team, the Team. The power of the team is invariably greater than the power of virtually any single individual.

3

You can almost never fully appreciate how important you are to the people you manage.

4

Great leaders consistently make good decisions.

5

You can't hit your targets yourself.

6

Learn from every experience.

7

Leave your ego at the door when you come into the office every morning.

8

No individual makes the puzzle.

ACKNOWLEDGMENTS

A big thanks to all those who have helped me on this journey. The book has gone through a number of iterations and, hopefully, there will be more in the future as I add ideas and new ways to help future leaders and managers.

When I started this project a few years ago I had help from Shanna, Walter, Pascal, Deborah, Louisa, Owen, Cody, John, Sophie, Damien, Gary, Cheryl, and Lucy.

Further on I had help from Bill, who did a great job editing, Dolores who did design, and John for the great caricatures and sketches. Not to forget Ken, who printed quite a few versions.

Throughout it all I have been helped by Maria, whose comments and insights never failed to improve each iteration. I'm pretty sure she's read the book more times than I have!

Finally, a thanks to Gareth at Cinematic, Ed at Severn Screen, and Julia at whitefox who have worked diligently to get this book into the hands of as many readers/listeners as possible.

Many thanks!

Henry

APPENDIX

Company Honors

Great Places to Work

Awards, by Country		2022
United Kingdom		4th
Canada	Halifax	4th
Italy	ConTe	4th
Spain	Admiral Seguros	2nd
France	L'olivier	7th
US	Elephant	GPTW accredited
	Compare	GPTW accredited
India	Admiral Technologies	GPTW accredited
	Admiral Solutions	35th
Europe		19th

Best Companies

Admiral is the only company to make this list every year since the award began in 2001.
- 2nd Best Big Company to Work For 2022
- Best Companies to Work For Special Award 2022—
  Wellbeing—1st

APPENDIX

- Best Companies to Work For Special Award 2022—Giving Something Back
- Best Companies to Work For Special Award 2022—Learning and Development
- Best Companies to Work For in Wales 2022—9th
- Best Insurance Company to Work For in the UK 2022—3rd
- Britain's Most Admired Companies—Britain's Most Admired Insurer—1st

Best Companies to Work For

Admiral is the only company to make the list every year since the award began in 2001.

Year	Place	Year	Place
2022	2nd	2011	9th
2021	5th	2010	16th
2020	3rd	2009	37th
2019	1st	2008	57th
2018	3rd	2007	21st
2017	2nd	2006	20th
2016	6th	2005	20th
2015	5th	2004	60th
2014	2nd	2003	46th
2013	11th	2002	42nd
2012	6th	2001	32nd

Best Companies to Work For

Special Awards

Year	Award
2021	Best Companies To Work For Special Award – Insurance's 10 Best Companies to Work For – 2nd Best Companies To Work For Special Award – 30 Best Companies to Work For in Wales – 7th Best Companies To Work For Special Award – Wellbeing – 1st
2020	Special recognition; Innovation in Engagement Practice
2019	Learning and Development; Best Leader, David Stevens
2018	Lifetime Achievement; Give Something Back; Best Leader, David Stevens
2017	Discovering Potential; Best Leader, David Stevens
2016	Best Leader, Henry Engelhardt
2015	Special recognition for 15 years; Best Leader, Henry Engelhardt
2014	Best Leader, Henry Engelhardt; Learning and Development

Prince's Trust
Million Makers Challenge

Year	Place
2018	Top 10
2017	2nd
2015	2nd
2014	3rd
2013	1st
2012	3rd
2011	2nd
2010	5th

Great Places to Work
World's Best Workplaces

Year	Place
2020	4th
2019	18th
2018	20th
2017	23rd

Other Awards
Best Workplace for Women in the UK

Year	Place
2022	3rd
2020	5th
2019	3rd
2018	3rd

United Kingdom's Best Workplaces

Admiral has made this list every year since the awards began in 2003.

Year	Place
2022	4th
2021	5th
2020	4th
2019	4th
2018	7th
2017	14th
2016	16th
2015	4th
2014	3rd
2013	2nd
2012	1st
2011	9th
2010	10th
2009	6th
2008	10th
2007	Top 10
2006	8th
2005	17th
2004	16th
2003	7th

Europe's Best Workplaces

Year	Place	Year	Place
2022	19th	2012	4th
2021	17th	2011	21st
2020	8th	2010	26th
2019	7th	2009	16th
2018	10th	2008	34th
2017	6th	2007	Top 100
2016	9th	2006	Top 100
2015	4th	2005	Top 100
2014	3rd	2004	Top 100
2013	2nd	2003	Top 100

INTERNATIONAL BEST WORKPLACE AWARDS
By Country

Canada

Admiral Insurance Services	2022	4th
Admiral Insurance Services	2021	5th
Admiral Insurance Services	2020	11th
Admiral Insurance Services	2018	13th
Admiral Insurance Services	2017	46th
Admiral Insurance Services	2016	34th
Admiral Insurance Services	2014	26th
Admiral Insurance Services	2012	14th
Admiral Insurance Services	2011	11th

France

France		
L'olivier	2023	6th
L'olivier	2022	7th
L'olivier	2021	6th
LeLynx	2021	14th
L'olivier	2020	11th
L'olivier	2019	25th
L'olivier	2018	38th
L'olivier	2017	35th
L'olivier	2016	19th
L'olivier	2015	22nd
LeLynx	2017	11th
LeLynx	2016	19th

Italy

Italy		
Conte.it	2022	4th
Conte.it	2020	4th
Conte.it	2019	3rd
Conte.it	2018	3rd
Conte.it	2017	2nd
Conte.it	2016	2nd
Conte.it	2015	9th
Conte.it	2014	11th
Conte.it	2013	9th
Conte.it	2012	8th
Conte.it	2011	11th
Conte.it	2010	22nd

India

India		
Admiral Solutions	2022	35th
Admiral Solutions	2021	64th
Admiral Technologies	2020	13th
IT–BPM, Admiral Technologies	2020	25th
Admiral Technologies	2019	7th
IT–BPM, Admiral Technologies	2019	35th
Admiral Technologies	2018	5th
IT–BPM, Admiral Technologies	2018	22nd
Admiral Technologies	2017	26th
IT–BPM, Admiral Technologies	2017	19th

Spain		
Admiral Seguros	2023	2nd
Admiral Seguros	2022	2nd
Admiral Seguros	2021	1st
Rastreator	2021	3rd
Rastreator	2020	6th
Admiral Seguros	2020	3rd
Rastreator	2019	6th
Rastreator	2018	6th
Rastreator	2016	4th
Rastreator	2014	5th
Rastreator	2013	4th
EUIGS	2018	8th
Admiral Seguros	2020	3rd
Admiral Seguros	2019	4th
Admiral Segruos	2018	4th
Admiral Seguros	2017	6th
Admiral Seguros	2016	7th
Admiral Seguros	2015	4th
Admiral Seguros	2014	8th
Admiral Seguros	2013	3rd
Admiral Seguros	2012	5th
Admiral Seguros	2011	10th
Admiral Seguros	2010	11th

Moneyfacts

Best car finance provider (shortlisted), 2023

Home insurance provider of the year (commended), 2023

Highly Commended Award, Best Loan Provider, *Insurance Times*

Direct Insurer of the Year, 2017

Inspire Awards from Learning and Work Institute, Wales

Large Employer of the Year, 2016, Wellbeing at Work

Responsible Business Award, 2016

Welsh Company of the Year 2005

National E-Commerce Award, Best Sales and Marketing, 2005

National Business Employer of the Year 2005

National Sales Awards

Bell, Best Inbound Call Centre, 2004, National Call Centre Awards, Bell, Best Small Call Centre, 2003

Welsh Business Achiever of the Year, 2002

Wales Quality Awards, Customer Satisfaction, 2001

National Customer Service Awards, Best Customer Service Manager (Jackie Miles), 2001

Welsh Contact Centre Awards, Best E-Commerce Initiative, elephant.co.uk, 2001

Welsh Company of the Year, 1999

Financial News, Excellence in Investment Banking

Small/midcap Deal of the Year, 2004, Personal Finance Awards

Admiral, Best Motor Insurance Provider, 2019; Admiral, Best Motor Insurance Provider, 2018; Admiral, Best Motor Insurance Provider, 2017; Admiral, Best Motor Insurance Provider, 2016; Admiral, Best Motor Insurance Provider, 2015; Admiral, Best Car Insurance Provider, 2014

Other Honors, North America

Virginia Business magazine, Best Places to Work, Admiral, 50th, 2021, Admiral, 18th, 2021, Admiral, 15th, 2021

Nova Scotia's Top Employers Admiral Insurance Services, 2015 Admiral Insurance Services, 2012

Halifax Chamber of Finance, Business of the Year

Admiral Insurance Services, finalist, 2015

Opportunity Now Excellence in Practice FTSE Female Pipeline Award, 2015

Best Workplaces in Canada for Women Admiral Insurance Services, 3rd, 2019 Admiral Insurance Services, 18th, 2014 Admiral Insurance Services, 18th, 2013 Admiral Insurance Services, 2nd, 2012 Admiral Insurance Services, 2nd, 2011

Special Awards, Best Workplaces in Canada, Admiral Insurance Services: for Inclusion (2020); Giving Back (2020); Mental Wellness (2018, 2019); Millennials (2018, 2019); Managed by Women (2019); Financial Services and Insurance (2017, 2018, 2019); 1000+ Employees (2018); World's Best

Workplaces (2017, 2018, 2019). Atlantic Canada's Top Employers Admiral Insurance Services, 2014 Admiral Insurance Services, 2012

Best Places to Work in Atlantic Canada Admiral Insurance Services, 26th, 2014 Admiral Insurance Services, 14th, 2012 Achievers 50 Most Engaged Workplaces in America, Admiral, 2012